Language Teaching Competences

Published in this series
Language Education Management

Language Teaching Competences
Richard Rossner

Language Course Management (forthcoming 2017)
Richard Rossner

Language Course Planning (forthcoming 2018)
Brian North, Mila Angelova, Elzbieta Jarosz,
Richard Rossner

Language Teaching Competences

Richard Rossner

OXFORD
UNIVERSITY PRESS

Great Clarendon Street, Oxford, OX2 6DP, United Kingdom

Oxford University Press is a department of the University of Oxford.
It furthers the University's objective of excellence in research, scholarship,
and education by publishing worldwide. Oxford is a registered trade
mark of Oxford University Press in the UK and in certain other
countries

© Oxford University Press 2017

The moral rights of the author have been asserted

First published in 2017

2021 2020 2019 2018 2017

10 9 8 7 6 5 4 3 2

ISBN: 978 0 19 440326 9

Printed in China

This book is printed on paper from certified and well-managed sources

ACKNOWLEDGEMENTS

*The author and publisher are grateful to those who have given permission
to reproduce the following extracts and adaptations of copyright material:*
p.38 Descriptors for 'Planning language teaching' from the
Cambridge English Teaching Framework (Cambridge English, 2014),
www.cambridgeenglish.org. p.15 'Reflective practice model of
professional educational development' from *Training Foreign Language
Teachers: A Reflective Approach* (1991) by Michael Wallace, Cambridge
University Press. p.45 Extracts from 'The BALEAP Competency
Framework for Teachers of English for Academic Purposes', 2008
and the 'BALEAP CPD Accreditation Scheme Handbook', 2004.
Reproduced by permission of the Chair of BALEAp. p.9 Extract from
The Language Teacher's Development by Dr Steve Mann (Centre for Applied
Linguistics, University of Warwick). Reproduced by permission of the
author. p.29 Extracts from 'European Portfolio for Student Teachers
of Languages' by David Newby et al., http://archive/ecml.at/Council
of Europe: © Council of Europe (ECML). Reproduced by permission.
p.43 Extract from 'European Framework for CLIL Teacher Education',
http://archive/ecml.at/Council of Europe: © Council of Europe (ECML).
Reproduced by permission. p.51 Extract from FREPA – A Framework
of Reference for Pluralistic Approaches to Languages and Cultures
– Competencies and resources', http://archive/ecml.at/Council of
Europe: © Council of Europe (ECML). Reproduced by permission. p.79
Definition of 'Methodology' from www.oxforddictionaries.com. By
permission of Oxford University Press, www.oup.com. p.140 Definition
of 'Competence' from www.oxforddictionaries.com. By permission of
Oxford University Press, www.oup.com. p.15 'Training foreign language
teachers: a reflective approach' by M. J. Wallace. Cambridge University
Press. p.36 © 2011 Education Services Australia Limited as the legal
entity for the COAG Education Council (Education Council). Oxford
University Press has reproduced extracts of the Australian Institute for
Teaching and School Leadership's Australian Professional Standards
for Teachers in this publication with permission from the copyright
owner. p.39 Extracts from 'Continuing Professional Development
(CPD) Framework for Teachers', https://www.teachingenglish.org.uk/
article/british-council-cpd-framework. Reproduced by permission of
the British Council. p.26 This material is taken from Michael Kelly and
Michael Grenfell, European Profile for Language Teacher Education: a
Frame of Reference, A Report to the European Commission Directorate
General for Education and Culture, September 2004. Written with the
assistance of Rebecca Allan, Christine Kriza and William McEvoy. There
are minor differences between the text of the Report and the text of the
summary version published by the University of Southampton (2004).
Both are available at: http://www.lang.soton.ac.uk/profile/

Although every effort has been made to trace and contact copyright
holders before publication, this has not been possible in some cases.
We apologize for any apparent infringement of copyright and if
notified, the publisher will be pleased to rectify any errors or omissions
at the earliest opportunity.

COVERED BY DISCLAIMER

http://www.et-foundation.co.uk/wp-content/uploads/2014

www.businessdictionary.com. Copyright © 2007–2011 Vijay Luthra and
BusinessDictionary.com. ALL RIGHTS RESERVED.

CONTENTS

ACKNOWLEDGEMENTS

This book, like the others in the series, would have been impossible without the work and commitment of many other people over several years. It is especially important to mention Brian North and Galya Mateva who, under the auspices of Eaquals, identified the potential of a 'profiling grid' for teachers and developed the first prototypes in 2005–6. A later version of the Eaquals Profiling Grid was used as a starting point for the project, co-funded by the European Commission, that developed the European Profiling Grid (EPG). As detailed in this book, the project involved individuals representing ten other organizations as well as Eaquals (represented by Brian North and myself). Major contributors to the project were Pernelle Benoit and Olivier Steffen as project co-ordinators on behalf of Centre International d'Etudes Pédagogiques; Karin Ende, Imke Mohr, and Rafael Deschka representing the Goethe Institut; Elena Verdía Lleó and Marta Higueras García representing the Instituto Cervantes, Spain; Tim Phillips, representing the British Council. Galya Mateva, on behalf of OPTIMA Bulgaria, was also closely involved in the project, and the sections of this book referring to the principles behind the EPG (in Part 1) and its uses (Part 4) are further developments of the work that Galya and OPTIMA Bulgaria led on the EPG user guide. Other people involved in the project included Helmut Renner (CEBS, Austria), Pierangela Diadori and Roberto Tomasetti (Università per Stranieri di Siena, Italy), Ludka Kotarska (ELS-Bell Education, Gdańsk, Poland), Aad Sinke (Hogeschool van Amsterdam), and Deniz Kurtoglu-Eken (Sabanci University, Istanbul). Deniz was also a member of the core team with whom I worked to develop the related Eaquals Framework for Language Teacher Training and Development, featured in Chapter 11. The other members of that group were Laura Muresan (QUEST Romania), Jim Ferguson and Sue Hackett (ACELS/QQI Ireland), Sharon Celtek (Sabanci University, Istanbul), Frank Heyworth (Eaquals), and Agnieszka Szplit (Jan Kochanowski University, Kielce, Poland). Some specific examples of reactions to and uses of the EPG are featured in Parts 2 and 4 of the book. Thanks for these are due to the following Eaquals member institutions: AVO Language and Examination Centre, Sofia; CA Institute of Languages, Brno, Czech Republic; EF Barcelona; Università per Stranieri di Siena (with the INDIRE research centre), Italy; and Università per Stranieri di Siena, Siena.

I would also like to express my gratitude to Tim Herdon, Tania Patterson, and Sarah Finch, who, on behalf of Oxford University Press, gave me unstinting advice and encouragement during the writing of this book.

INTRODUCTION

Background

Language teaching and learning is an ever more crucial part of education worldwide. The days when foreign languages were mainly the pursuit of enthusiasts are gone; today, most policy-makers and other **stakeholders** in education have a clear understanding of the power and importance of languages in education and of the cognitive, social, and professional value of learning other languages. The accelerating pace of globalization means that being able to use more than one language has become much more important for further and higher education, as well as for employment. Globalization also brings with it an ever greater and ever more evident need for intercultural understanding and communication to facilitate positive and productive participation in international social groups, and in conversations that span boundaries of language and culture.

Purpose of this series

An abundance of books and other media has been produced for teachers, as well as for **teacher trainers**, but there are very few publications offering practical guidance for those with managerial responsibilities in language education. The three books in the *Language Education Management* series aim to fill this gap by making coherent and practical contributions which draw on the accumulated expertise and resources of Eaquals. They each focus on one of three important and interrelated areas of language education:

- the development of language teaching competences
- the management of language education programmes
- the planning of language education courses.

About the series

The *Language Education Management* series and the related website materials bring to a wider public the know-how, tools, and guidelines developed within Eaquals and its network of partners. The three books in the series are not intended to be academic studies and do not contain exhaustive overviews of the existing literature. They are designed to provide practical guidance and opportunities for reflection for anyone with management, supervisory, and training roles in the field of language education.

There are three guiding principles behind the series. The first is a belief that, since language plays such a crucial role in all education, and more and more education takes place in languages that are not the students' first language (L1), there is a need for foreign language education to be more closely integrated with education across the **curriculum**. The second is that all foreign languages are to be viewed as equal: English may be more widely learned and spoken than other languages, but this does not mean that the methods and approaches used by teachers of English as a foreign language should somehow serve as models for other languages, or that educators and students in English-speaking countries can afford to be less committed to foreign language learning. The third principle is that, while in the areas of language education covered by this series there may be no 'right answers', there is a great deal of good practice to draw on, and a continual need to seek opportunities to further enhance the quality of language education, both in the classroom and through the systems and resources that support teaching and teachers' **professional development**.

With these principles in mind, each book in the series contains background information and practical guidance, as well as tasks which encourage reflection on the ways in which that guidance can best be followed or adapted. Most of the questions in the reflection tasks have no 'right answers', since the best way forward usually depends on the specific characteristics of an educational context. The aim of these tasks is to stimulate readers to think about the suggestions offered in relation to their own experiences and needs.

About this book

Language Teaching Competences, the first book in the series, focuses on the **European Profiling Grid** (**EPG**) and its role in helping teachers to develop their **competences**. This involves first exploring key issues around teacher development at individual and team level, and then examining in detail the principles, content, and possible uses of the EPG, as well as considering other such tools that have been developed to describe and support the development of teaching competences.

Part 1 introduces some key terms and concepts, in order to define the meanings of the terms as used in this book. Part 2 begins with a review of several frameworks of different kinds for language teachers specifically and also those for teachers in general. It then considers how the EPG came about and explains the thinking and principles behind it, before examining how it is organized and what it contains. Part 3 then provides a detailed overview of each of the categories of competence covered in the EPG. Part 4 focuses on how the EPG and its digital version, the e-Grid, can be used by teachers, by their managers, and by teacher trainers and mentors. Finally, Part 5 focuses on the related and more detailed **Eaquals Framework for Language Teacher Training and Development** (**Eaquals TD framework**), to raise some important general points and offer advice on how to use any such framework.

Additional resources can be found on the accompanying website: www.oup.com/elt/teacher/ltc

PART ONE

1 WHY THIS BOOK?

Introduction

Like all teachers, language teachers face daily challenges, however strong their motivation. Some challenges are exhilarating: preparing to teach a new class or a new type of course; being asked to design some new resources; or being invited to be a **mentor** to a less experienced colleague. These experiences can be exciting and fulfilling. But more often than not, teachers face less positive challenges such as flagging student motivation, the need to help them prepare for a high-stakes exam, or having to manage classes that are too large and/or too infrequent to allow learners to make meaningful progress. Almost all such experiences, including the less positive ones, contribute in some way, usually unconsciously, to a teacher's **professional development**. The purpose of this book is to explore ways in which language teachers can engage consciously with their own individual development in a planned and reflective manner, using the support of tools such as competence frameworks and, depending on the circumstances, in co-operation with their mentors or trainers and their managers.

Activity 1.1

If you are or have been a teacher:

Think of two or three experiences in your teaching that you found especially motivating. What made them special? Did they affect your development as a teacher or your attitude to teaching? How?

Think of one or two experiences in your teaching that you found upsetting or demotivating. What made them upsetting or demotivating? How did you handle these situations? Did they have any long-term impact on your teaching?

Diversity of contexts and challenges

Language teachers work in an enormous range of educational contexts—arguably more so than teachers in any other field, especially in an increasingly globalized world. The teaching contexts range from preschool, where learners can be as young as two years of age, to postgraduate courses at university and corporate training programmes for executives. While the majority of language teachers are found in **mainstream schools** and work with students between the ages of five and eighteen, many others work in the private sector and provide courses for young learners and teenagers after school, or for adults who want or need to improve their language skills for work, study, or travel. In addition, language learning has a crucial role to play in the integration of migrants and refugees in the host society, and in many areas of vocational education.

At the time of writing, there are institutions certified against Eaquals' high standards in 33 countries. Consider the different demands made of language teachers in the following fictitious situations:

Institution A is in France. The students are adults of all ages, but mostly in their twenties; they come from various countries and wish to learn French. They come for between two and thirty-six weeks and study around five hours daily. A teacher teaches the same class all day for at least four weeks. There is a maximum of ten students in a class.

Institution B is in Greece. It is the language department of a mainstream private school providing English, German, and French courses. Teachers teach students between the ages of four and eighteen for a few hours a week. The methodology until now has been grammar-oriented but, due to changes in Ministry of Education requirements, a shift to a more communicative approach and **curriculum** is being made. Students at higher levels also prepare for international exams. There are up to 25 students in a class.

Institution C is in Switzerland. It provides courses exclusively for companies, including banks, insurance companies, and the post office. Its courses take place early in the day during working hours on company premises. The classes are often taught one-to-one or in groups of no more than three students. The content of teaching depends on what the company has requested, which may be quite specialized.

Institution D is in Spain. It offers English courses in six different locations to adults and young learners. Courses normally involve three hours of class time per week, and class sizes are no more than fourteen students. At lunchtime the same teachers are often asked to go to private mainstream schools to provide additional English lessons for children between five and eleven years of age. Here class sizes vary, but the rooms are big enough for 30 students. Some teachers may also be asked to go to company premises to teach employees in small groups.

Institution E is a language centre in a Turkish university. Students are in degree programmes in international business or international relations; their English classes take place alongside their degree courses. Language learning includes a focus on academic skills such as **critical thinking**, researching information, putting forward persuasive arguments, and giving presentations. All students have to pass a test in English as part of their degree. Group sizes can be up to 20 students.

| **Activity 1.2** | In your opinion, which of the institutions above offers the most challenging teaching context and which the most professionally rewarding? Why? |

A language teacher's work can be more or less challenging, and also more or less intrinsically rewarding, for a number of reasons. Here are some of them:

- The number of different groups to be taught has an impact on the amount of preparation and marking to be done, especially if the groups are different in terms of language level, age, or composition. Groups are also quite often based in different locations. All of these factors make working at Institution D demanding.

- The number of students in a class is a factor: more students may mean more management challenges and more **learning styles** and expectations to take into account. Having said this, one-to-one classes and very small groups (as in Institution C) may also be challenging in terms of planning and motivation, and the need to travel frequently from one teaching venue to another may be a physical challenge.

- Whether the group is monolingual or plurilingual (as in Institution A) makes quite a difference. On the one hand, the need for a 'common language' makes the **target language** a natural, if not an essential, choice. On the other hand, cultural sensitivity is important, as is an ability to deal with very different language learning issues relating to students' different first languages (L1s).

- The intensity of the course and whether the students are studying in a country where the target language is spoken can make a considerable difference to the amount of progress that can be made. In general, because the courses are intensive and held in a country where the target language is spoken, students in an institution like Institution A will learn the language more quickly than those studying it for a few hours a week in an institution where their L1 is spoken. However, if students are staying for different lengths of time, the composition of the class and the needs of learners may frequently change.

- Working in a mainstream school (as in Institution B), where the language lessons are not frequent and take place according to a curriculum which may be crowded with up to ten other subjects, may place special demands on teachers. This is even more the case if teachers are asked to teach a subject through a foreign language, such as in a **Content and Language Integrated Learning (CLIL)** context.

- Teaching in an Institution like Institution E may be especially challenging because of the need to work out exactly what kind of language and academic skills support individual students need, and to find or develop tasks that are appropriate for the purpose.

It should also be remembered that, in many countries where part-time work is common and teachers' salaries are low, a teacher may take on work at two or more different institutions with diverse student populations and curricula. This situation adds its own challenges and potentially its own professional (as well as financial) rewards.

How language teachers are made

There are many reasons why people choose to become language teachers, including a love for the language being taught, a sense of vocation as a teacher, and, especially in the case of teachers of English, the opportunity to 'see the world'. It is surprising to find how many language teachers have a background that is unrelated to teaching or language: teachers often have prior careers as engineers, lawyers, administrators, and graphic designers; many language teachers have stories to tell about their decision to go into language education. It is also common for language teachers to see language teaching as a temporary episode in their career, even a stopgap, although that does not stop many of them 'catching the bug' once they experience the enjoyment of interacting with students in the way that supporting the learning of another language requires.

Like those of any subject, novice language teachers instinctively follow the model of teaching set by their own teachers, especially those they consider the 'best', and they bring their own temperament, interpersonal skills, and habits to this model. A 'deep-end' experience, where no training is provided before teaching begins, can be tough. But many survive it and go on to 'learn by teaching', even if some of those early habits adapted from their own experiences as learners become entrenched features of their teaching persona.

A more common route into language teaching is by completing a university degree in the target language (or more than one language) and a teacher training or 'pedagogy' module. Depending on the language and country, training to become a teacher may involve supervised teaching practice, whereby the would-be teacher experiences the reality of managing a lesson with 'real' students and is given **feedback** by a trainer or supervisor. Given the demand for teachers of English, a common pathway for them, whatever their higher education background, is a course lasting just 120 hours (often completed in four weeks), which includes a few hours of supervised teaching practice; the **Cambridge English CELTA** and the **Trinity CertTESOL** are two examples of this kind of course. This intensive training focuses more on the practicalities of language teaching—materials, methods, techniques, classroom management, etc.—than on theory. Those who successfully go through this training often praise its effectiveness, however short the time was for exploration and reflection, and however restricted the recipes for effective teaching may have been.

| **Activity 1.3** | How and why did you become a language teacher? What are the similarities and differences between your story and those of other language teachers you know? What kind of training did you receive? Do you think it prepared you well for a teaching career? If so, why? If not, what was lacking? |

In all cases, once a teacher has taken on a teaching position (or more than one), there is little time available for further on-the-job training and even less for other kinds of professional development. It is clear that most teaching takes place behind closed doors. The best and more or less the only independent judges of a teacher's effectiveness are their own students, and opinions may vary from student to student. Comprehensible and 'uncoloured' feedback from students is usually hard to obtain, and feedback from other observers—whether supervisors, peers, or trainers—is usually very infrequent.

The focus of this book

This book is essentially about quality and effectiveness in language teaching. It is based on experience of working with and talking to many language teachers, in different countries, and in a range of diverse educational contexts, over many years. Its starting point is that, whatever factors drew someone into the language teaching profession, whatever training they had to start with and have had since, and however experienced they may be, there will be a latent desire to develop further as a language teaching professional and to provide support for learning that is even more effective, and more consistently so. Most of a teacher's working hours are spent actually preparing and teaching in classrooms without the company or support of colleagues. In terms of professional contact with colleagues, teachers are sometimes solitary people. Teachers may have little day-to-day opportunity to engage consciously in professional development or to consider what aspects of their teaching have been really effective, or less effective. Under such circumstances, it is hard for them to engage consistently and with enthusiasm in self-development, but it is important—indeed essential—to do so, and to seek whatever means are available to support that development.

The role of Eaquals

Eaquals, as an international association of institutions and people with a belief in the necessity and practical possibility of developing quality in all areas of language education, is fundamentally a 'community of practice' defined as 'groups of people who share a concern or a passion for something they do and learn how to do it better as they interact regularly' (Wenger-Trayner & Wenger-Trayner, 2015). We also believe that teachers should belong to at least one community of practice, and that they should use it as a key means of furthering their own development.

Conclusion

This book aims to offer practical suggestions and guidelines for language teachers and those working with them on how to further professional development. It will focus on raising awareness, **self-assessment**, and **reflection** as key activities, and it will explore how one of the most widely used frameworks describing language teaching competences can serve as a tool and a springboard.

2 TERMINOLOGY AND BACKGROUND

Introduction

The fields of language teaching and **teacher development** involve various terms and concepts, some of which can be used in more than one way and overlap with others. This chapter will discuss some key terms used in this book and the way they should be understood here.

Some basic terms

Activity 2.1

Which of the following statements do you agree with more? Why?

Teacher development should mainly be the responsibility of individual teachers, with their employer providing support and opportunities as well as guidance.

Employers of teachers should take responsibility for the development of their teachers, and teachers should participate in and contribute to the professional development activities provided.

Steve Mann (2005) identifies some key features of teacher development in his article 'The Language Teacher's Development':

- It is in principle a **bottom-up** process, so it can be contrasted with **staff development** organized by the institution, which is a **top-down** process.
- It values the view of the teacher as an insider rather than the view of outsiders such as **inspectors**.
- It is independent of the organization but often functions more successfully with the institution's support and recognition.
- It is a process which can never be finished (i.e. teachers, however experienced, can always develop further).
- It is a process of articulating and reflecting on inner conscious choices in response to the outer world of the teaching context.
- It is wider than 'professional development', as it includes personal, moral, and value dimensions.
- It can be encouraged and integrated in both training and education programmes.

Some important contrasts, described in more detail below, arise from this view of teacher development involving numerous terms and different kinds of experience that all contribute to, but are not the same as, teacher development.

Teacher training/teacher education

Teacher training is a term usually reserved for short practical courses, such as the 120-hour Cambridge English CELTA or Trinity CertTESOL courses (and various other even shorter courses), offered for would-be and novice teachers of English as a foreign language. **Teacher education**, on the other hand, implies a longer-term structured programme, such as one leading to an initial teacher qualification (commonly at least one year in higher education) and involving supervised teaching practice, or a course taken after first gaining experience as a teacher—typically a post-graduate course or specialized modules within a master's degree programme. Courses leading to qualifications like the Cambridge or Trinity College diplomas for teachers of English as a foreign language can also be included in this category. For both teacher training and teacher education, some kind of assessment is required to check whether participants have met the necessary requirements to 'pass' the course.

In-service training

In-service training (**INSET**) is likely to be designed to cope with the needs, which are often diverse, of a group of teachers working within an institution. It may take various forms, and typically does not lead to a formal qualification: staff workshops, for example, on specific aspects of language teaching such as handling errors or focusing on pronunciation, or short courses on a given topic, such as teaching young learners and using **ICT** in the classroom.

Staff development/continuing professional development

This is a much broader term; it may include INSET activities, but it may also include, for example, a programme of peer observation, observation by mentors focusing on specific areas of teaching, reading groups, or small classroom research projects. Staff development implies that activities are also organized to address the development needs of other members of staff, not just teachers. For example, managers may have the opportunity to attend workshops on management topics such as team building, time management, and so on, and workshops on cultural awareness or customer relations may be offered to administrative staff. Staff development is often referred to as **continuing professional development** (**CPD**), which adds two important features: it is (or should be) ongoing, hence the choice of the word 'continuing'; and it focuses on the knowledge and skills required for the profession—which is, in this case, teaching, and specifically language teaching.

Teacher development

Teacher development is, by implication, the responsibility of individual teachers. It is not the same as INSET organized by an institution or CPD, which might imply that an institution or a director of studies intends to develop the staff they supervise. This transitive use of 'develop', whereby an institution or individual develops another person or group of people, can be contrasted with the intransitive use, whereby an individual develops professionally of their own accord. Crucially, teacher development is therefore more comprehensive and potentially broader in scope and impact than CPD or INSET. Mann points out that professional development is 'career orientated and has a narrower, more instrumental and utilitarian remit' whereas teacher development is 'more inclusive of personal and moral dimensions' (Mann, 2005, p. 104). The impact of teacher development is also long-lasting, indeed lifelong, in a way that INSET organized by an institution alone is not. Although teachers in an institution also develop as a team, each individual in the team will develop in different ways and directions, and developments may take place in a different order and at a different speed. It is hard to take account of this in CPD or INSET that involves groups of individuals. On the other hand, group activities within CPD or INSET are additional and very valuable means by which individuals develop.

Let us consider the case of a fictitious teacher, Anna. During her working life as a language teacher, various events and activities will take place which contribute to her development as a teacher, probably starting with an initial teacher education course. As Anna's career as a teacher progresses, she has various other learning experiences. Some are organized by her employers, such as INSET workshops, observations, or reading groups; others are sought out and undertaken by Anna herself, such as attending an external conference, or experimenting with new resources that she has created; and others still are activities which she and her colleagues have engaged in together, such as peer observation and classroom research. All of these together, combined with her ongoing experience as a teacher, contribute to her development, as do other things such as collaborating with another teacher on a project or feedback from students.

If teacher development is the responsibility of the teacher concerned, it is necessarily individual. But this does not prevent teacher development from being facilitated by activities such as INSET, CPD, or teacher education—quite the contrary. As individuals, we take different insights from these collective activities, and we develop in diverse ways.

Activity 2.2   How do these aspects of teacher development relate to your own situation and the way teacher development is viewed in your institution?

Mann (2005) also raises another point that teacher development can often go beyond the professional field. While we tend to think of personality traits in adults as fixed and unchanging, experienced **teacher trainers** and teachers know that they change on a personal level all the time: they become more or less patient, shy, assertive; better or worse listeners; funnier or more serious; and so on. So the question is: are we aware of these often imperceptible personal changes, and do these changes lead to more effective teaching?

Key factors in teacher development

Activity 2.3   Consider the development pathways of two fictitious teachers working in the same institution, Abigail and Jean-Pierre (see Figure 2.1). Both have been there for four years now. Rank the events and activities for each teacher in order according to the impact they are likely to have had on their development (1 = highest impact). Then add notes on the ways in which they may have developed as a result of each event or activity, and explain why.

	Abigail	**Jean-Pierre**
Before starting to teach	Three-year language degree at university and a four-week course with supervised teaching practice.	A four-year law degree and three years' experience working in a lawyer's office; two weeks of intensive training at the institution. No initial teacher training.
During their first year	• Taught groups of adults at three different levels and groups of young children at two different levels. • Was observed by the director of studies three times in the first month and given feedback. • Observed three different colleagues teaching children	• Taught a group of adults at intermediate level and five small groups of company employees. • Was observed six times in the first two weeks as part of his **induction** and was given feedback. • Did team-teaching for two months with someone with more experience of in-company teaching. • Wrote some teaching/learning materials for a group of three lawyers he was teaching.
INSET	Attends about six different workshops organized by the school each year.	Has so far attended only four workshops at the school due to timetable conflicts and travel.
Other activities	• Has been involved in online CPD with ten colleagues from four different countries. They have read and discussed several articles about different aspects of teaching. • Regularly observes two colleagues and is observed by them, with discussion following.	• Has attended conferences run by the national teachers' association, and has given a presentation about teaching the language to lawyers. • Has used his mobile to record himself teaching in-company, and has discussed the recordings with the director of studies and the training director at the company. • Has started a master's degree in language teaching.
New responsibilities	Is involved in organizing testing and assessment activities for young learners.	Mentors and observes another teacher who has never done in-company teaching before.

Figure 2.1 Development pathways of two teachers

Activity 2.4	Make a short list of what you consider to be the most important areas of knowledge, skills, and personal characteristics that constitute competence as a language teacher.

Competence

Competence is complicated to define. Noam Chomsky (1965) famously distinguished between linguistic 'competence' and linguistic 'performance' (i.e. between knowledge of a language and its use in a specific context). His work focused on the internal and external processes that make it possible for us to use a language in the myriad ways we do. Competence is made manifest through performance in any **domain**, including that of language. Crucially, however, performance is also affected by a range of factors such as the context, the performer's state of mind, challenges of the subject matter or task, etc. This means that competence is only made manifest to the extent that is made possible by a performance at a given moment in time. For example, musical competence is measured by a musician's ability to perform to a certain level of skill and virtuosity in playing an instrument or singing. It may be that, because of a number of factors at play, the performance either does not do justice to the musician's level of competence, or it is at a level above what would normally be expected of a musician with that level of competence.

A distinction is made in a literature review concerning the professional development of teachers, published by the EU Commission, between <u>teaching</u> competences, the practical competences needed to work with students in classrooms, and <u>teacher</u> competences, which include all those competences that teachers require to do their job, including classroom related competences (EU Commission 2011, pp. 7–8). In this book, for the sake of simplicity and consistency with the main frameworks referred to, teaching competences will be used to encompass both these categories of competence.

To measure language teaching competence, we look for the ways in which activities and tasks in the classroom are handled by the teacher, how students are managed and monitored, how the target language is used by the teacher, and how successfully these skills support learning. Behind these practical skills observed in the 'performance' of the teacher, there is the knowledge, understanding, and a range of technical skills acquired through teacher education and training, as well as the additional awareness and skills accumulated through experience. However, teaching competence is more complicated than this. It is certainly the case that teachers make choices based on their knowledge and skills. But, in addition, underlying both knowledge and skills, there are a set of values or principles related to personal attitudes (to society, education, language, culture, etc.) that have evolved throughout the teacher's personal development from childhood onwards. It is the way in which these elements interact that determines the effectiveness of a given teacher's performance in a specific lesson. A schematic diagram of this view of teaching competence is shown in Figure 2.2.

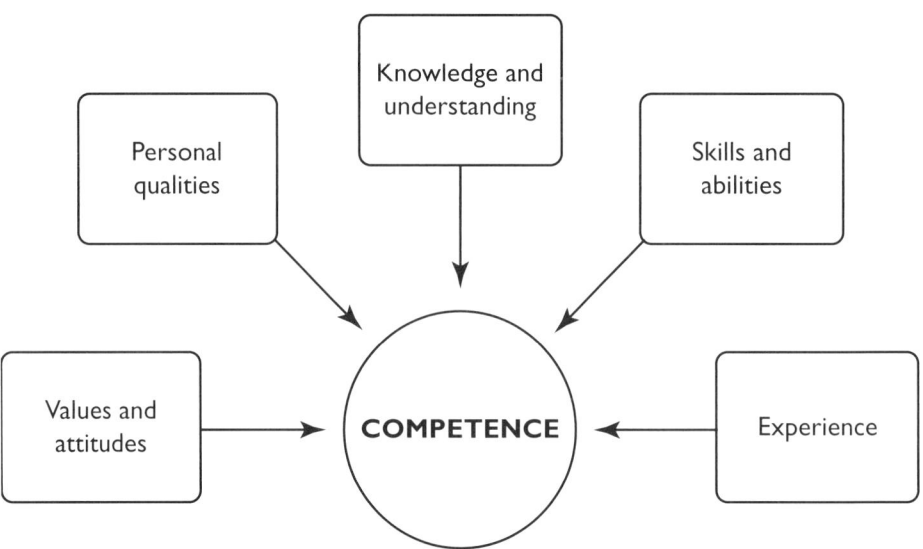

Figure 2.2 Contributors to teaching competence

A note on the teacher as 'performer': teaching, the main purpose of which is to support learning, is unlike musical or theatrical performance, although it is not uncommon to see teachers playing a role and entertaining their students during a lesson. Crucially, teaching (of any subject) involves social, interactive, and communicative competences of a kind quite different from those needed by musicians or actors.

Of course, all of these elements of teaching competence interact with one another, and not all of them are easily distinguishable. So, in some respects, 'teaching competences' may be hard to assess. Nevertheless, it is important that they be assessed in order to make sure all aspects of development are addressed.

Activity 2.5   Think of two teachers you know well and have observed teaching. How does each of the factors in Figure 2.2 contribute to their current level of competence as a teacher? What are the key differences between them in terms of these factors? Which of them do you consider 'stronger' in each area?

In language education, the main purpose of teacher education, teacher training, INSET, and CPD is to enable teachers to develop or further develop the competences they are most likely to need as teachers in order to enable them to be as effective as possible in supporting and stimulating language learning. Teacher development is what enables individual teachers to take what they have gained from CPD, INSET, and other development or training activities, as well as their ongoing teaching experience, and to tailor it to their personal values and qualities, to fulfil the requirements of the educational contexts they work in, and to meet the needs of the students they work with. Being a teacher is not like being an artist, but one would not expect a group of artists who have acquired roughly the same knowledge, know-how, and technical abilities through similar education and training in fine art to paint or draw in the same, or even in similar, ways. The 'art' of teaching involves consolidating one's uniquely individual qualities and experiences with the knowledge and professional skills acquired.

Reflection

Activity 2.6	Consider the quotation below, attributed to the Chinese philosopher, Confucius. Do you agree with his view of how we learn wisdom in general and, in relation to language education, wisdom about teaching? 'By three methods we may learn wisdom: first, by reflection, which is noblest; second, by imitation, which is easiest; and third by experience, which is the bitterest.'

Development of any kind (whether personal, professional, economic, or cultural) depends in large part on an ability to reflect on one's experiences, and on one's successes and failures, in order to be able to identify changes and adjustments that might be advantageous; these may, for example, concern one's actions and behaviour, deployment of skills, energy and enthusiasm, and styles of interaction. This is especially true in any kind of learning situation—and teacher development is all about learning. In Training Foreign Language Teachers: A Reflective Approach (1991), Michael Wallace provided a schematic model of **reflective practice**, shown in Figure 2.3. According to this model, reflection is seen as crucial for the continual development of competence. One's prior experience, existing beliefs and 'mental constructs', and knowledge received from training and reading are continually reflected upon and subtly developed in the light of daily practice as a teacher or **trainee teacher**. The model is linear in structure, but the ongoing process of reflecting on practice is cyclical and continuous, leading to progressive changes in one's 'mental constructs' and the gradual evolution of one's competence.

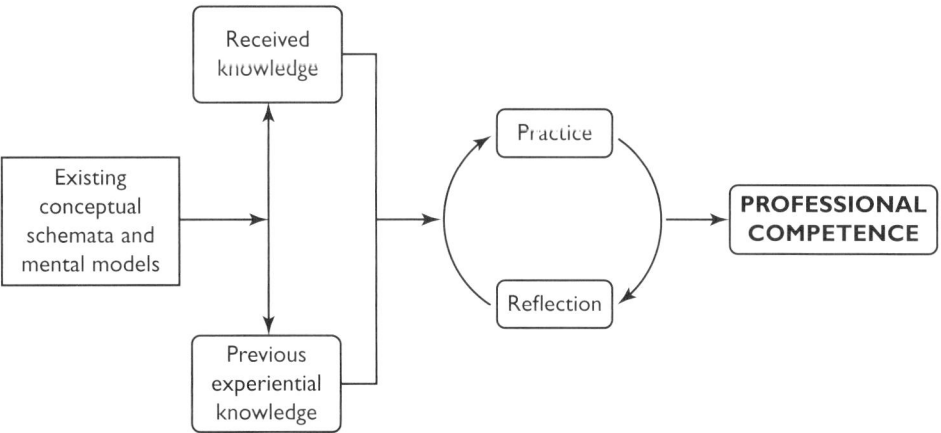

Figure 2.3 Schematic model of 'reflective practice' (adapted from Wallace, 1991)

An important point about this kind of reflective practice is that it is not just a matter of dwelling on past experiences in a discouraged way or feeling good about past successes. Most importantly (and less emotionally), it involves reflecting on future possibilities, ways of building on success and/or ways of overcoming disappointing experiences. What can one do in future to be more successful? What are the options for development in one's practice?

Activity 2.7	Think of an incident in classroom teaching that really made you reflect and change or develop your beliefs about some aspect of language teaching and learning. What happened? Did it also lead to some development in your competence as a teacher? In what way?

Reflection on a successful or less successful lesson, the outcome of a discussion with students, the results of a test, a discussion with colleagues, and so on, happens regardless, whether in a structured and thoughtful way based on 'the evidence', or in a hasty, gut-reaction manner based on immediate feelings and impressions. The key point is whether any clear thoughts arise from the process of reflecting on whether things could be done differently in future, how they might be done differently, and how significant or experimental the changes being considered would be. The kind of reflection that results in desperation and gloomy thoughts about whether one can ever be effective as a teacher, at least in that class, is not likely to be productive. In Chapter 9, we will discuss whether there are simple guidelines to follow to ensure that reflection is constructive and useful, such as ensuring that there is good evidence to focus on during reflective practice, and that there are opportunities to discuss the outcomes of reflection (see Walsh & Mann, 2015). It will also look at the symbiotic relationship between individual reflective practice and collective reflection, whereby colleagues work together to draw lessons from their reflection.

Role of the institution and teachers in teacher development

It was noted above that, while teacher development should be a bottom-up process and primarily the concern of individual teachers, the institutions teachers work for can also make very important contributions to it (see page 11). There are various ways in which institutions, in particular academic managers and co-ordinators who work closely with teachers, can help to ensure that teacher development at a collective and individual level is rich, broad, and beneficial to individual teachers, to their learners, and thus to the institution itself. These include: awareness-raising and consultation; assessment and the encouragement of self-assessment; internal mentoring; and the organization and/or financing of INSET and CPD events. Academic management in language education, including the active support for teacher development, is discussed in more detail in the companion volume in this series: *Language Course Management.*

Awareness-raising and consultation

Activity 2.8	When new teachers join your institution, how is the institution's approach to teacher development explained to them? How is the topic of teacher development introduced, and what roles do teachers and managers play in it?

Earlier in this chapter, definitions of and distinctions between teacher development, INSET, CPD, and teacher education were proposed. Before communicating with teachers about teacher development, it is important that managers within institutions formulate and agree on terminology and their philosophy and approach to this crucial area, including the support that teachers can expect to receive and the responsibilities of teachers themselves in relation to teacher development. In encouraging an open dialogue with teachers, it is best to be flexible and to invite teachers, including newly arriving teachers, to comment on and contribute to the institution's philosophy of approach to teacher development.

Within any institution, teacher development will entail action and reflection on the part of both individual teachers and the institution. It is therefore crucial to be clear about the support and intervention that teachers individually and collectively can expect from their managers and supervisors, and about what managers expect from teachers, bearing in mind that some of them may be employed on a part-time, short-term, or ad hoc basis, and that they may also work for other employers.

Activity 2.9	If you are a teacher:
	Ideally, how would you wish your employers to support your development? What different forms would you want the support to take?
	If you are a manager or supervisor:
	Ideally, how would you consult teachers about their development, and what approach would you encourage them to take?

Collaboration and a spirit of shared endeavour are key to successful teacher development. Some teachers and managers will have more experience in certain areas than others, but this does not mean that less experienced colleagues will have nothing to contribute to group CPD activities and INSET. The rest of this chapter will discuss the ways in which assessment, especially self-assessment, and reflection, can contribute to meaningful professional growth on both the individual and team level.

Assessment and self-assessment

What is 'assessment'? This term is one of a cluster around making judgements or, at the very least, estimations. Aside from 'judgement' and 'estimation', the cluster also includes the terms 'evaluation', 'measurement', and 'testing'. All of these imply a process of finding and considering evidence in order to determine whether a given person, product, or service meets certain criteria. Several questions arise from this:

- What are the criteria for assessment, and where did they come from?
- What evidence has been collected, and how was this done?
- Based on the evidence, who determines whether the criteria are met?
- What is the impact of this judgement, and who or what is affected?

Assessment can be more or less formal, and more or less high stakes (i.e. significant in terms of impact). It is important for the degree of formality to match the purposes and intended outcomes of the assessment. For example, the assessment of students taking a final examination which has consequences for future studies or work is usually formal since the stakes are high. Assessment of how a group of students have progressed in a given period may be less formal because the low-stakes purpose (although still important) is to review how the course is going as input for the planning of the next period of teaching. It is likely that no one will be penalized or rewarded.

Activity 2.10   Have you ever assessed someone's teaching? If so, how did you carry out the assessment? What criteria and what evidence did you use for the assessment? What was the purpose of the assessment?

As well as valid and appropriate tools and transparent and agreed procedures, assessment of teaching and self-assessment by teachers play a very important role in identifying teacher development priorities at an individual and team level.

Assessment by others

People assess teaching competences for different reasons. Three common reasons are as follows:

- as support for professional development (including the professional development of the person doing the assessment)

- as part of quality assurance, i.e. to check whether the teaching being assessed is up to the standard agreed within an institution and is adequately supporting the learning that students are engaged in

- as a means of deciding whether a teacher on a course leading to a qualification is competent enough to pass and receive a diploma or certificate.

In this book, we are mainly concerned with the first reason and its potential role in the broader scope of teacher development. There are two key issues to address in relation to this kind of assessment: first, in assessing a teacher's performance, the observer may consciously or unconsciously make a judgement without referring to any criteria; second, the criteria used or the focus points suggested in observation forms are often arbitrary or representative of the observer's subjective views. This is not to diminish the importance of **focused observation**, where, in advance of the lesson, some specific aspects of the teacher's performance to be focused on have been identified, perhaps at the teacher's request.

Activity 2.11	A university language centre has 25 teachers on full-time or part-time contracts and 15 others who are engaged on a flexible basis and paid hourly. These 40 teachers teach five different languages between them. Some full-time/part-time teachers also have roles as co-ordinators and mentors for their respective languages. Eva was recently appointed as the full-time director of studies at the language centre. She needs to quickly gain an insight into the general quality of language teaching at the language centre and to get a picture of the level of competence of the various teachers in order to prepare a professional development plan for the coming year. In your opinion, how could she best do this?

Heads of department who are responsible for managing a team of teachers and for checking quality quite often assess teaching with both quality assurance and developmental objectives in mind. After all, while quality standards for teaching and the support of learning are intended to be institution-wide, teachers are individuals with different ways of using their competences and with differing individual professional strengths and development needs.

Other people who may assess teaching competences for various purposes include:

- colleagues wishing to compare their own practice with that of the teacher they are observing (and implicitly assessing) and to learn from the experience, or who are invited or asked as mentors to give feedback on the teaching of a colleague who is perhaps less experienced or is new to the institution

- those in a training role, whose concern is mainly individual development and training but may also be concerned with the standards required to successfully complete, for example, an INSET course

- external advisors or inspectors, checking that the institution meets formal requirements or quality standards

- students, who make instinctive and usually private assessments of the teaching they experience, and are frequently asked to give an opinion at the end of a course.

The assessments of any of the above **stakeholders** can have a marked impact on teachers' views of themselves as professionals, and indeed on their employers' opinion of their competence and, consequently, on teacher development.

Self-assessment

Perhaps the most important kind of assessment of teaching is that done by teachers themselves about their own performance. For teacher development to be genuine and effective, teachers need to develop an awareness and understanding of their own competence and their strengths and weaknesses as a teacher, and to form a view that is as clear as possible of what works well in their teaching and what is less effective. Much more will be said about this in Chapters 6–9.

Successful self-assessment involves, at the very least, the following:

- a willingness to develop an all-round awareness of one's teaching competences and teaching persona
- some sort of framework or criteria to serve as a basis for reviewing one's performance and estimating one's competence as a teacher
- good evidence of what actually happened and how effective it was
- an ability to reflect on the evidence in the light of the framework used, and to draw some conclusions that are unclouded by emotion.

Activity 2.12

Have you tried to assess your own teaching? How did you do it?
Was it easy or difficult? Why?
What evidence did you base your assessment on?
What kind of framework or criteria did you refer to?
What was the outcome of your self-assessment?

Sources of evidence for self-assessment

Self-assessment can play a big part in teacher development, and there are various possible sources of evidence to draw on. These include:

- **self-observation**, for example on video or audio recordings made during teaching; this is one of the most comprehensive and informative sources, but it requires some setting up
- a reflective diary outlining main events and reactions
- feedback gathered from students during or after a lesson
- the results of a test or some other assessment mechanism (for example, task-based assessment) used with students
- feedback from someone observing you
- your own recollection of a lesson and reflection on how well it went.

Generally speaking, two or more sources of evidence combined will provide a better basis for self-assessment than a single source, since they may point in different directions. For example, students may have said they enjoyed the lesson and learned a lot, but when you see the video of it, you may feel there were many missed opportunities or too much intervention on your part.

Activity 2.13

In your past or current teaching contexts, which of the above sources of evidence would be easiest to use? Can you think of any others? Do you use or have you used any of them for self-assessment purposes?

Criteria for self-assessment

Self-assessment, or indeed assessment of someone else's teaching, is not easy without some clear criteria or a framework of focus points to work with. Most language teaching institutions have a system for regularly observing teachers, and forms or checklists for recording salient aspects of the teaching observed may be part of that system. For example, the form may ask the observer to note whether the teacher started the lesson on time, whether he or she worked with all students in the class (not just the strongest or most vocal), whether he or she used **group work** and **pair work** effectively, and so on. Such focus points are relevant in different ways, and even if there are dozens of them, they are unlikely to capture the 'whole story' of a lesson. The headings are often devised by the institution or to suit the needs of the observer, though in some cases specific points are agreed beforehand with the teacher being observed. The issues around observation are discussed in detail in the companion volume in this series *Language Course Management*. Chapter 4 of this book describes a profiling grid designed to provide a more complete and explicit set of **descriptors** of language teaching competence so as to offer a single frame of reference for teachers when assessing themselves, as well as for those assessing the teaching of others.

Reflection on self-assessment, and possible outcomes

Teaching is a demanding and complex profession involving continual interaction with learners. The kinds of questions teachers, including language teachers, are likely to ask themselves when assessing their own performance will relate to the following:

- their effectiveness ('Am I doing a good job?', 'Was that a successful lesson?')
- their learners' well-being and learning ('Are my students progressing?', 'Are they motivated?', 'What works best for them as a group and as individuals?')
- future planning ('Do I need to change what I'm doing?', 'What adjustments do I need to make to plans for upcoming lessons?', 'Do I need to try something new with these learners or that individual learner?').

The trick is to learn to assess oneself without undue pessimism or optimism and a maximum of realism, over an extended period of time, such as a semester or a year, more than once. This is more likely to lead to useful questions to do with individual professional development ('Are there areas where I need to grow in competence and/or confidence?', 'Do I need help with this? What kind of help?').

How managers can help with self-assessment

There are many reasons why teachers working in an institution may not normally assess their own competence in a conscious and meaningful way. Teachers are, after all, busy people with lots to preoccupy them both in and outside the classroom. Lesson preparation is a considerable challenge, and many teaching jobs involve a certain amount of administration. So self-assessment may be limited to vague and sporadic reflection on what has just happened, thoughts and feelings about certain students, and the good and not-so-good aspects of teaching certain courses or classes. If this is the case, it is important to have discussions about teacher development which raise awareness of the value of self-assessment, and to provide suggestions on how to engage in it effectively. This can be made more convincing if people in the discussion can cite their own experiences of self-assessment. An example might be a situation where an academic co-ordinator shows clips from a video of herself teaching, mentions some of the reactions she had as she watched it, and invites teachers to note strong and not so strong points.

Another reason why self-assessment may not be standard practice is the absence of any kind of frame of reference for it. Unless some criteria are selected or developed by the institution, it is likely that self-assessment will be avoided altogether, or focus mainly on imprecise and subjective feelings about what teachers feel they do well and what they are not so good at.

Activity 2.14	Lack of time and lack of a frame of reference have been identified as two reasons why teachers might not engage in self-assessment. Think of two or three more reasons why you or teachers you have worked with do not normally assess themselves.

A useful way of getting teachers to at least try out self-assessment is to show how it could fit into a wider system of support, including, for example, the institution's procedures for deciding on knowledge, skills, and issues to be addressed in group CPD events and INSET. The key point is that teachers' views of their own individual development needs, combined with institutional priorities and the opinions of academic managers, are likely to lead to more appropriate support for teacher development and enable managers to demonstrate a commitment to individual development as well as the development of the team.

Conclusion

This chapter has considered some concepts and terms that will come up frequently throughout the rest of this book, such as 'teacher development', 'CPD', 'competence', 'self-assessment', and 'reflection'. The intention was not to suggest that these are the only possible interpretations of these terms but to clarify the way in which they will be used in subsequent chapters.

The final part of this chapter began to consider the role employers and managers of teachers can play in supporting development activities and in assisting with individual and collective teacher development.

PART TWO

3

COMPETENCE FRAMEWORKS

Introduction

The idea of specifying and describing teaching competences is not new. Indeed, competence frameworks exist for many professions and specific roles, such as managers and healthcare workers, as well as teachers. The concept can be traced back to at least 1982 and a study in the USA on the competences required for management, the purpose of which was 'to determine which characteristics of managers are related to effective performance in a variety of management jobs in a variety of organizations' (Boyatzis, 1982, p. 8). The key feature of this study is the linking of 'characteristics' with 'effective performance', applicable to more or less any job.

There is a discussion of the value of competence frameworks for teachers in *Supporting Teacher Competence Development for Better Learning Outcomes* (European Commission, 2013). In answer to the question 'Why define teaching competences?', the following reasons are suggested, among others:

- the desire to enhance the quality or effectiveness of education
- the need to make the teaching profession more attractive and provide for career progression
- the desire to promote teachers' lifelong learning and engagement in continuing professional development
- the demand for the professionalization of teaching
- the desire to clarify teachers' roles
- the growing importance of the role of school leadership
- the need to assess the quality of teaching.

This book goes on to provide examples of work done in the area of teaching competences from around the EU, with a strong emphasis on continuing professional development and lifelong learning. These are seen as key elements in the EU's **Education and Training 2020 strategy** (see Website references).

This chapter explores the purposes, form, and content of a variety of frameworks for teaching competences, both in general education and language education, developed by a diverse range of organizations for a variety of teaching contexts.

Some of these date back ten years or more and were influential in the thinking behind the **European Profiling Grid** (**EPG**) (see Website references). The aim is to explore the scope and intended uses of these tools and how they relate to the concepts discussed in Chapter 2.

Frameworks related to initial teacher education

The European Profile

The European Profile for Language Teacher Education (commonly known as the European Profile) is the result of a project supported by the European Commission and co-ordinated by The University of Southampton. It focuses on bringing together the expertise of institutions in Europe to generate a set of recommendations concerning the aims, structure, and content of initial teacher education and INSET. As detailed in the final report (Kelly et al., 2004), the focus of the European Profile is more on specifying the coverage that would be desirable in teacher education courses than on specifying in detail the knowledge and skills to be developed. This is understandable given the diverse ways in which such courses are structured and run across Europe.

The European Profile is based on a survey of pre-service teacher education courses and case studies. It summarizes conclusions reached by the project team about the required structure and contents of such courses in the form of a list of 40 **indicators**, which are divided into four sections:

- structure, i.e. the way in which pre-service teacher education for language teachers should be organized (for example, 'the opportunity to observe or participate in teaching in more than one country')
- knowledge and understanding (for example, 'training in language teaching methodologies, and in state-of-the-art classroom techniques and activities')
- strategies and skills (for example, 'training in methods of learning to learn')
- values (for example, 'training in team-working, collaboration and networking, inside and outside the immediate school context').

Figure 3.1, which shows one of the eight indicators in the 'knowledge and understanding' section, is a sample of how each of the 40 indicators in the European Profile is presented.

---

19. Training in the application of various assessment procedures and ways of recording learners' progress

Trainees have a comparative view of the advantages and disadvantages of various assessment methods and are aware of the criteria that affect methods of assessment.

Trainees are able to adapt different ways of **recording learners' progress** and analyse the strengths and weaknesses of a range of methods.

Trainees use **oral** and **written** tests or exams, **summative assessment**, written **project-based work**, **continuous assessment**, practical projects, group projects and portfolios.

They understand which assessment techniques to use to best display the learners' progress accurately in the area in which they are interested.

Trainees learn to record all results and interpret them to chart the learner's progress in a meaningful way. This will also allow them to see areas in which the learner may need to make improvements. The use of commonly understood levels, such as those in the Common European Framework (CEF) is extremely valuable.

Strategies for Implementation and Application

↘ Teaching trainees about assessment procedures and recording learners' progress can take place during trainees' language proficiency courses. By integrating improvement of trainees' language proficiency and awareness of methods of assessment, trainees develop a more cyclical view of teaching, learning and assessment.

↘ Trainees are given the chance to witness formal and informal assessment procedures during their school-based experience.

↘ Trainees need to conform to the assessment procedures in place in their school. However, there is often scope for developing new methods of assessment, or treating existing ones flexibly.

Figure 3.1 The European Profile (excerpt from Kelly and Grenfell, 2005)

Figure 3.1 suggests strategies for how the 'knowledge and understanding' section specified in more detail in the two descriptors can be handled in the context of a teacher education course. However, it might be argued that the competences described require a lot more knowledge, understanding, and practical professional skill than is detailed here.

Activity 3.1   Read the 'Strategies for Implementation and Application' box in Figure 3.1. Were these strategies used in your initial teacher education course or in a subsequent course? How well developed do you consider your competence to be in the areas of assessment and recording learners' progress?

The 40 indicators listed in the European Profile are backed up by detailed case studies (available in the appendices to the European Profile—see Website references). These were carried out with the co-operation of 11 partner organizations, mainly universities, in ten countries across Europe. In each case study, examples are given of the ways in which some of the indicators are applied in practice on the teacher education courses run by the institutions.

The appendices also contain a useful set of quality assurance and enhancement guidelines for each indicator in the European Profile. Figure 3.2 provides an example of these guidelines, applied for the indicator shown in Figure 3.1.

Educational Aims:

- To introduce you to the teacher's role in formal assessment procedures.
- To develop knowledge of the benefits of different informal assessment techniques that can be employed in the classroom.
- To enable you to assess your learners correctly and record their progress in a meaningful manner.
- To introduce you to the scales of the Common European Framework and encourage you to use them to assess the four aspects of language (reading, writing, speaking, and listening).

Intended Learning Outcomes:

a) Knowledge and Understanding
- You will have a repertoire of assessment procedures which you can use flexibly according to the particular setting. These include, for example, written and oral tests, group work presentations, and continuous assessment.
- You will understand which of these techniques to use to best display the learners' progress in the area in which you are interested.
- You will be able to record all results and interpret them to chart the learner's progress in a meaningful way. This will also allow you to see areas in which the learner is weak and where more work needs to be done.

b) Transferable Skills:
- You will be able to record accurately and interpret statistical information.
- You will be able to apply a number of assessment techniques to your teaching when necessary.

Checklist:

What they do:
- Trainees are introduced to formal assessment procedures. They understand how the marks of formal assessment have to be recorded and the procedures surrounding this.
- Trainees are familiar with a repertoire of assessment techniques and understand the contexts in which different techniques are appropriate.
- Trainees understand how to use an assessment technique to obtain accurate results.

How they do it:
- Trainees can use tools such as the Common European Framework scales to assess their own language proficiency accurately. They then can use them to assess the language proficiency of their learners.
- Trainees understand the advantages of different assessment techniques and are able to select a technique appropriate to what they are hoping to test.

> How they know they do it:
> • During the school experience, trainees will have the opportunity to assess learners.
> • Trainees critically evaluate the benefits of one particular assessment technique over another in a given context and can justify their reasons.
> • Trainees can interpret the results of assessment of a group of learners and use this to inform their teaching.

Figure 3.2 Training in the application of various assessment procedures and ways of recording learners' progress (Kelly & Grenfell, 2005)

Activity 3.2   Look at the checklist in Figure 3.2 and the intended learning outcomes. Which of the outcomes and points in the checklist would you consider to be also relevant to experienced teachers undertaking CPD or INSET? How can they be used with such teachers in focused observation and/or self-assessment?

If we disregard the emphasis on trainees in the European Portfolio guidelines, it is clear that parts of the list would be a useful resource for experienced teachers to use either for self-assessment or in observation. Indeed, the heading 'How they know they do it' in itself implies self-assessment or reflection on practical teaching. It is also worth noting that, as in the **Eaquals Framework for Language Teacher Training and Development** (**Eaquals TD framework**) (see Website references), knowledge and understanding are separated from transferable skills, although in the 'How they do it' section the two are intermingled. For example, 'understanding the factors which influence a learner's learning' is followed by 'an ability to recognize the needs of … learners,' which is followed by 'an ability to adapt … teaching to the needs of the learners.' However, as the guidelines were primarily intended for pre-service trainees and their tutors, there is no indication of the degree of understanding or ability required at different phases in a teacher's development, as there is in the EPG or the Eaquals TD Framework.

The European portfolio for student teachers of languages

Another tool concerned mainly with initial education for language teachers is the European Portfolio for Student Teachers of Languages, (EPOSTL), which was developed with the support of the **European Centre for Modern Languages** (**ECML**) (see Website references). This was designed as a portfolio—that is, a document in which trainee teachers in initial teacher education record their progress. Its coverage is extensive, as is made apparent in Figure 3.3 which shows an overview of the areas of EPOSTL, and overlaps with that of both the European Profile and the Eaquals TD Framework.

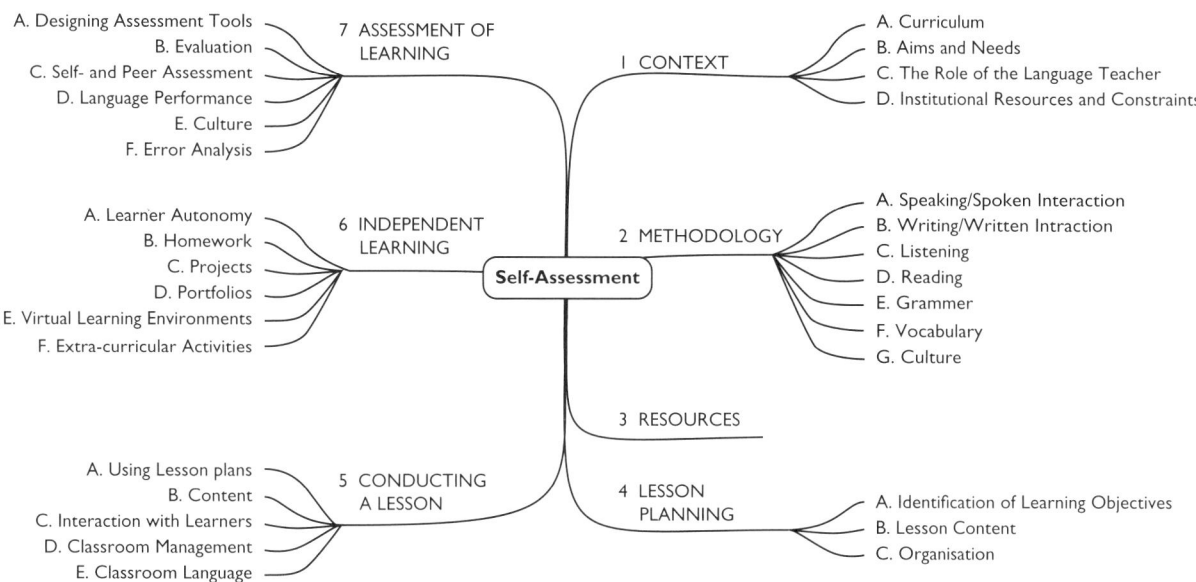

Figure 3.3 Mind map of the areas covered by EPOSTL (ECML, 2006)

Addressing trainee teachers, the introduction to EPOSTL states:

> It will encourage you to reflect on your didactic knowledge and skills necessary to teach languages, help you to assess your own didactic competences and enable you to monitor your progress and to record your experiences of teaching during the course of your teacher education.
> (ECML, 2006, p. 5)

As shown in Figure 3.4, EPOSTL includes descriptors in the form of can-do statements relating to context, methodology, resources, lesson planning, conducting a lesson, independent learning, and the assessment of learning. The emphasis of these can-do statements is mainly on the trainee's ability to take into account various factors relating to students' needs and motivation, as well as the needs of other stakeholders such as employers and parents/carers. There is less emphasis on practical ability, because the focus is on planning. EPOSTL partly overcomes the problem of the degree of understanding or ability through its design. The idea is that trainee teachers periodically assess themselves and gradually fill in the horizontal, arrow progress bar to indicate how they feel they are doing in relation to each of the descriptors.

> # EPOSTL   SELF ASSESSMENT
>
> **B.   Aims and Needs**
>
> 1.   I can understand the personal, intellectual and cultural value of learning other languages.
>
> 2.   I can take account of overall, long-term aims based on needs and expectations.
>
> 3.   I can take into account differing motivations for learning another language.
>
> 4.   I can take into account the cognitive needs of learners (problem solving, drive for communication, acquiring knowledge etc.).
>
> 5.   I can take into account the affective needs of learners (sense of achievement, enjoyment etc.).
>
> 6.   I can take into account and assess the expectations and impact of educational stakeholders (employers, parents, funding agencies etc.).
>
> 7.   I can take into account attainment target levels set in curricula (e.g. deriving from the *Common European Framework of Reference*).

Figure 3.4 Subsection on aims and needs from the section on context in EPOSTL (Newby et al., 2006)

| **Activity 3.3** | Compare Figure 3.4 with Figure 3.2 (see page 27). Which areas of understanding or ability are covered in the European Profile but not in EPOSTL, and which areas are covered in EPOSTL but not in the European Profile? |

Even though the European Profile and EPOSTL are aimed primarily at the same kind of trainees participating in initial teacher education, there are clear differences of emphasis in these two excerpts covering closely related areas. For example, the European Profile guidelines shown in Figure 3.2 include reference to special educational needs and learning a language for vocational purposes, whereas the sample from EPOSTL in Figure 3.4 makes reference to cognitive needs and motivation, which are not specifically referred to in this part of the European Profile. This might lead one to the conclusion that it would be wise to combine the indicators and can-do statements in both of these framework documents and also those in other frameworks, such as the Eaquals TD Framework, in order to achieve comprehensive coverage. However, the purposes of each framework are different: the European Profile is aimed at teacher trainers, whilst EPOSTL is a portfolio for trainee teachers to use during their initial teacher education courses. It is also true that there are many ways of looking at language teaching, which depend partly on the views, experiences, and aims of those who create the respective frameworks. The question as to how analytical and comprehensive such frameworks can be is discussed later on in this chapter.

A key aim of EPOSTL is to encourage self-assessment and reflection, thereby developing strategies during initial teacher education that are essential for practising teachers, however experienced they are. The topic of self-assessment will be covered in more detail in Chapter 9, where guidance is offered on the use of the EPG for this purpose.

| **Activity 3.4** | Look at the sample from EPOSTL in Figure 3.5. What evidence would a teacher or trainee teacher need in order to be able to complete the progress bar in a meaningful way? How useful would a portfolio like EPOSTL have been to you in your initial training or when you first started working as a qualified teacher? How useful could it be to an experienced teacher? |

EPOSTL
SELF ASSESSMENT

A.   Speaking/Spoken Interaction

1.   I can create a supportive atmosphere that invites learners to take part in speaking activities.

2.   I can evaluate and select meaningful speaking and interactional activities to encourage learners of differing abilities to participate.

3.   I can evaluate and select meaningful speaking and interactional activities to encourage learners to express their opinions, identity, culture etc.

4.   I can evaluate and select a range of meaningful speaking and interactional activities to develop fluency (discussion, role play, problem solving etc.).

5.   I can evaluate and select different activities to help learners to become aware of and use different text types (telephone conversations, transactions, speeches etc.).

6.   I can evaluate and select a variety of materials to stimulate speaking activities (visual aids, texts, authentic materials etc.).

7.   I can evaluate and select activities which help learners to participate in ongoing spoken exchanges (conversations, transactions etc.) and to initiate or respond to utterances appropriately.

8.   I can evaluate and select various activities to help learners to identify and use typical features of spoken language (informal language, fillers etc.).

Figure 3.5 A sample from EPOSTL (Newby et al., 2006)

Frameworks for teachers in mainstream education

State authorities in various countries have developed standards or frameworks for teachers working in mainstream schools and colleges. There are important differences of emphasis in the way such standards can be used, as the European Commission has identified:

> 'In educational policies, two contrasting approaches about standards can be found: a bureaucratic, technical approach for accountability purposes, focused on measuring, monitoring, comparing and regulating individual behaviour; or a developmental approach, with loose definitions of competences indicative of performance, stressing principles and codes of practice.'
>
> (European Commission, 2013, p. 16)

Frameworks of competence can and often do form the basis of such standards, and the style and contents of the framework often indicate how bureaucratic and technical or developmental they are intended to be. We will consider two examples: the Australian Professional Standards for Teachers (AITSL, 2011), and the New Overarching Professional Standards for Teachers, Tutors, and Trainers in the Lifelong Learning Sector developed by Lifelong Learning (LLUK, 2007). As with most of the frameworks examined in this book, these two frameworks can be seen as instruments both for articulating what is expected of teachers professionally on the one hand, and providing a stimulus for professional development on the other.

Comparing the AITSL and LLUK professional standards

The standards in the AITSL framework are divided into three main domains of teaching: 'professional knowledge', 'professional practice', and 'professional engagement', each of which has been divided into subcategories. The descriptors are organized over four successive professional levels: 'graduate', 'proficient', 'highly accomplished', and 'lead'.

In contrast, the standards in the LLUK framework (now superseded by a much less comprehensive standard) are divided into six domains:

- professional values and practice
- learning and teaching
- specialist learning and teaching
- planning for learning
- assessment for learning
- access and progression.

Each domain is divided into subcategories covering professional values, professional knowledge and understanding, and professional practice, akin to the domains in the AITSL framework and roughly equivalent to the 'knowledge and understanding', 'skills and abilities', and 'values and attitudes' contributors to teaching competence proposed in Figure 2.2 (see page 14). However, it is worth noting that there is no gradation across career stages in the LLUK framework, as these are seen as equally relevant for all teachers working in the lifelong learning sector in the UK, wherever they are in their careers. Figure 3.6 provides an example of how this works.

Domain D: Planning for learning

The values set out in Domain A support and inform all the commitments, knowledge and practice set out in the other domains.

PROFESSIONAL VALUES

Teachers in the lifelong learning sector value:

AS 1 Learners, their progress and development, their learning goals and aspirations and the experience they bring to their learning.

AS 2 Learning, its potential to benefit people emotionally, intellectually, socially and economically, and its contribution to community sustainability.

AS 3 Equality, diversity and inclusion in relation to learners, the workforce, and the community.

AS 4 Reflection and evaluation of their own practice and their continuing professional development as teachers.

AS 5 Collaboration with other individuals, groups and/or organisations with a legitimate interest in the progress and development of learners.

They are committed to:

DS 1 Planning to promote equality, support diversity and to meet the aims and learning needs of learners.

DS 2 Learner participation in the planning of learning.

DS 3 Evaluation of own effectiveness in planning learning.

PROFESSIONAL KNOWLEDGE AND UNDERSTANDING	PROFESSIONAL PRACTICE
Teachers in the lifelong learning sector know and understand:	*Teachers in the lifelong learning sector:*
DK 1.1 How to plan appropriate, effective, coherent and inclusive learning programmes that promote equality and engage with diversity.	DP 1.1 Plan coherent and inclusive learning programmes that meet learners' needs and curriculum requirements, promote equality and engage with diversity effectively.
DK 1.2 How to plan a teaching session.	DP 1.2 Plan teaching sessions which meet the aims and needs of individual learners and groups, using a variety of resources, including new and emerging technologies.
DK 1.3 Strategies for flexibility in planning and delivery.	DP 1.3 Prepare flexible session plans to adjust to the individual needs of learners.

DK 2.1 The importance of including learners in the planning process.	DP 2.1 Plan for opportunities for learner feedback to inform planning and practice.
DK 2.2 Ways to negotiate appropriate individual goals with learners.	DP 2.2 Negotiate and record appropriate learning goals and strategies with learners.
DK 3.1 Ways to evaluate own role and performance in planning learning.	DP 3.1 Evaluate the success of planned learning activities.
DK 3.2 Ways to evaluate own role and performance as a member of a team in planning learning.	DP 3.2 Evaluate the effectiveness of own contributions to planning as a member of a team.

Figure 3.6 Excerpt from the LLUK professional standards framework (LLUK, 2007, pp. 10–11)

Activity 3.5

Read through the three domains in Figure 3.6. How important do you think it is that teachers should be asked to reflect on their values and professional commitment (labelled 'AS' and 'DS' in this example), and to relate these to their professional knowledge and practice ('DK' and 'DP')? Would you personally find a standard presented in this form useful?

The standards exemplified in Figure 3.6 are quite demanding but fairly generic in terms of the values, which are worthy but applicable to most areas of teaching, not only planning. The 'commitments', 'professional knowledge', and 'professional practice' subcategories are more closely focused on planning but do not go into detail about methods and techniques of planning or stages of planning—as is the case, for example, with EPOSTL and other frameworks more focused on teacher education and professional development.

Activity 3.6

Look at Figure 3.7, which shows an excerpt from the AITSL professional standards which focuses on planning, and answer the following questions:

• Which of the standards in Figure 3.7, if any, do you consider are not applicable to language teaching?
• If you are a teacher, assess yourself against these standards and reflect on whether the related career stage is appropriate.
• Compare Figures 3.6 and 3.7. Which of the two examples do you think is clearer and more useful? Why?

The standards in Figure 3.7 are not underpinned by values and commitments as in the LLUK example in Figure 3.6. On the other hand, while being generic rather than detailed, they map out a fairly clear career progression for teachers across four stages.

Standard 3 – Plan for and implement effective teaching and learning

Focus area	Graduate	Proficient	Highly Accomplished	Lead
3.1 Establish challenging learning goals	Set learning goals that provide achievable challenges for students of varying abilities and characteristics.	Set explicit, challenging and achievable learning goals for all students.	Develop a culture of high expectations for all students by modelling and setting challenging learning goals.	Demonstrate exemplary practice and high expectations and lead colleagues to encourage students to pursue challenging goals in all aspects of their education.
3.2 Plan, structure and sequence learning programs	Plan lesson sequences using knowledge of student learning, content and effective teaching strategies.	Plan and implement well-structured learning and teaching programs or lesson sequences that engage students and promote learning.	Work with colleagues to plan, evaluate and modify learning and teaching programs to create productive learning environments that engage all students.	Exhibit exemplary practice and lead colleagues to plan, implement and review the effectiveness of their learning and teaching programs to develop students' knowledge, understanding and skills.
3.3 Use teaching strategies	Include a range of teaching strategies	Select and use relevant teaching strategies to develop knowledge, skills, problem solving and critical and creative thinking.	Support colleagues to select and apply effective teaching strategies to develop knowledge, skills, problem solving and critical and creative thinking.	Work with colleagues to review, modify and expand their repertoire of teaching strategies to enable students to use knowledge, skills, problem solving and critical and creative thinking.
3.4 Select and use resources	Demonstrate knowledge of a range of resources, including ICT, that engage students in their learning.	Select and/or create and use a range of resources, including ICT, to engage students in their learning.	Assist colleagues to create, select and use a wide range of resources, including ICT, to engage students in their learning.	Model exemplary skills and lead colleagues in selecting, creating and evaluating resources, including ICT, for application by teachers within or beyond the school.

Figure 3.7 Excerpt from the AITSL professional standards framework (AITSL, copyright Education Services Australia, 2011)

Other frameworks

Several frameworks of different kinds have been published for practising language teachers. Some focus on national contexts or specific specialisms, while others are general and international in scope, like the EPG itself. For example, the European Centre for Modern Languages is running a project as part of their 2016–19 programme and one of the objectives is to create a user guide that would serve as a comprehensive reference tool for existing frameworks of teacher competences, providing a stepping stone towards considering the feasibility and usefulness of an overarching framework, and covering all the key competences required for language teaching. The initial research carried out by the project team identified a list of 27 frameworks, standards, and checklists for language teachers within Europe.

General frameworks for teachers

Let us consider two frameworks that were published after the appearance of the EPG, one for English language teachers and the other for teachers working in CLIL contexts.

Cambridge English Teaching Framework

The Cambridge English Teaching Framework (see Website references) is similar to the AITSL framework discussed above in that descriptors of competences are provided across four stages of teacher development, labelled 'foundation', 'developing', 'proficient', and 'expert'. The descriptors cover five main categories of competence that, because of the greater focus on the learner and on language knowledge and awareness, are rather different from those encompassed by the other frameworks considered in this book. The five main categories of competence are:

- learning and the learner
- teaching, learning and assessment
- language ability
- language knowledge and awareness
- professional development and values.

While the first two focus on pedagogic issues, the third and fourth categories are concerned with language ability and awareness. The fifth category (like the fourth category of the EPG described in Chapter 8), concerns the teacher's role as a professional, including attitudes to observation, participation in CPD activities, and teamwork with other colleagues. Figure 3.8 shows an example of one complete subcategory in the 'teaching, learning and assessment' category.

2. TEACHING, LEARNING and ASSESSMENT

2.1 Planning language learning

	Foundation	Developing	Proficient	Expert
Lesson planning	• Has a basic understanding of some key principles of lesson planning, and uses this understanding to plan basic systems and skills lessons according to a given template with basic awareness of learners' needs and difficulties and some linking of activities within a lesson. • Usually follows the lesson plan without much adaptation, may not yet be able to respond to unforeseen classroom events, and has started to see some clear links between planning and teaching choices and subsequent student learning.	• Has a reasonable understanding of many key principles of lesson planning and uses this understanding to plan reasonably detailed systems and skills lessons according to a given template with some awareness of learners' needs and difficulties and some linking of activities within one/ more lessons. • Sometimes adapts the lesson plan according to the flow of the lesson, is able to respond to some unforeseen classroom events, and can see some clear links between planning and teaching choices and subsequent student learning.	• Has a good understanding of many key principles of lesson planning, and uses this understanding to plan detailed systems, skills and integrated lessons according to their own template, with good awareness of learners' needs and difficulties and linking of activities within/across a series of lessons. • Adapts the lesson plan where necessary, is able to respond appropriately to most unforeseen classroom events, and can see clear links between planning and teaching choices and subsequent student learning.	• Has a sophisticated understanding of key principles of lesson planning and uses this understanding to plan detailed and sophisticated systems, skills and integrated lessons (often unconsciously without the need for detailed plans and has internalised sufficient routines and resources), with a clear rationale and thorough understanding of learners' needs and difficulties and linking activities across a number of lessons to support learners and their learning. • Adapts the lesson plan where necessary, is able to respond appropriately, confidently and automatically to almost all unforeseen classroom events and has developed a sophisticated understanding of the link between planning and teaching choices and subsequent student learning.
Course planning	• Has a basic understanding of some key principles of course planning. • Is able to plan a short series of lessons with simple links between them.	• Has a reasonable understanding of many key principles of course planning. • Is able to plan a series of lessons with clear links between them.	• Has a good understanding of many key principles of course planning. • Is able to plan a series of lessons and/or a whole course which meet the requirements of a prescribed syllabus.	• Has a sophisticated understanding of key principles of course planning. • Is able to plan a series of lessons and/or whole course in a creative and sophisticated way, and is able to work creatively within the constraints of a prescribed syllabus.

Figure 3.8 Descriptors for 'Planning language teaching' from the Cambridge English Teaching Framework (Cambridge English, 2014)

One of the main purposes of the Cambridge English Teaching Framework is to enable teachers or trainee teachers to relate their own level to the various teacher training certificates and examinations that Cambridge English offers, such as the Cambridge English CELTA and the **Teaching Knowledge Test**.

British Council CPD Framework

Like the AITSL framework (see page 36) and the Cambridge English Teaching Framework reviewed above, the British Council Continuing Professional Development (CPD) Framework for teachers (see Website references) envisages teachers acquiring competence in professional practices over four stages of development, but with a different, more cognitive emphasis. These are shown in Figure 3.9.

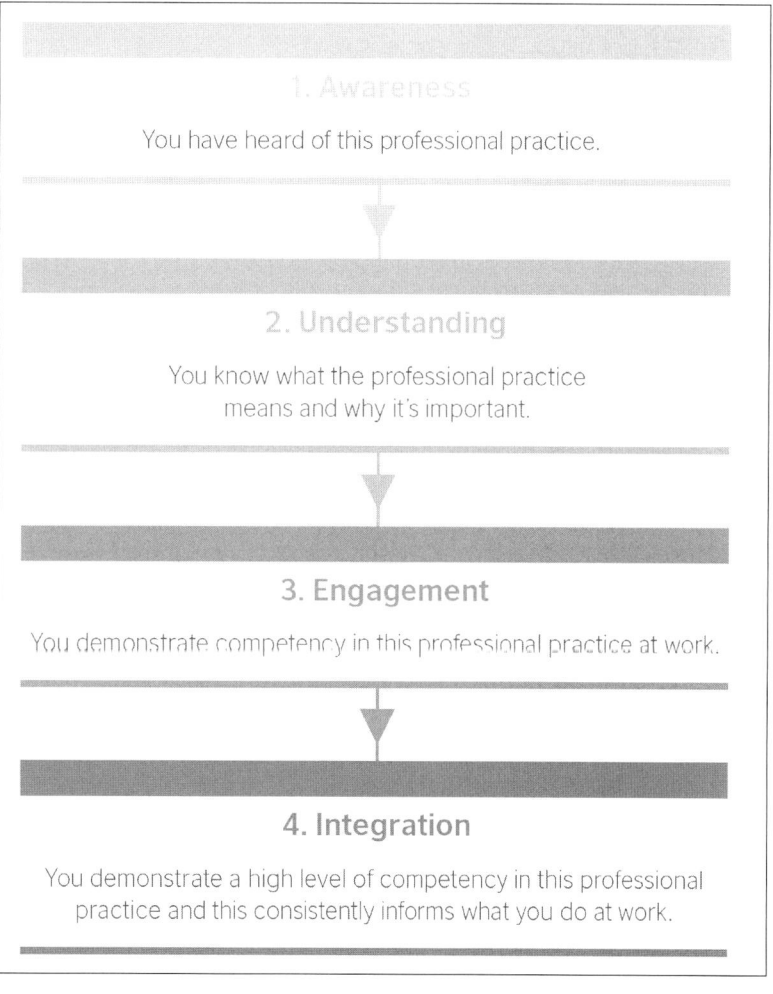

Figure 3.9 Stages of development in the British Council CPD Framework (British Council, www.teachingenglish.org.uk)

Instead of descriptors like those in the Cambridge English Teaching Framework, the British Council CPD Framework contains a list of what each professional practice involves, like that shown in Figure 3.10.

Understanding learners

Understanding learners involves the following elements:

Making decisions about teaching and assessment by applying an understanding of the following learner characteristics:
- level of attainment
- age
- interests
- preferred ways of learning
- group dynamics
- motivation to learn, both generally and in relation to specific subjects
- educational, social, cultural and linguistic background
- any special educational needs
- level of autonomy
- personality.

Exploring theories of learning and applying them to my context and learners.

Conducting needs analyses and applying the results.

Applying an understanding of the impact of the learning environment on my learners.

Reflecting on my approach to understanding my learners and the impact this has on their learning.

Figure 3.10 Sample list of elements from the British Council CPD Framework (British Council, www.teachingenglish.org.uk)

Comparing the British Council CPD and Cambridge English Teaching Frameworks

Activity 3.7   Compare the two lists of categories in Figures 3.11 and 3.12. What differences in emphasis and approach to English language teaching competences are there between the two frameworks? What could be the reasons behind these differences?

British Council CPD Framework

Planning lessons and courses
Understanding learners
Managing the lesson
Knowing the subject
Managing resources
Assessing learning
Integrating ICT
Taking responsibility for professional development
Using inclusive practices
Using multilingual approaches
Promoting 21st century skills
Understanding educational policies and practices

Figure 3.11 Summary of the areas of competence covered by the British Council CPD Framework

Cambridge English Teaching Framework
Learning theories
Foreign and second language acquisition
Language teaching methodologies
Understanding learners
Lesson planning
Course planning
Selecting, adapting, supplementing and using learning materials
Using teaching aids
Using digital resources
Creating and maintaining a constructive learning environment
Responding to learners
Setting up and managing classroom activities
Providing feedback on learner language
Teaching vocabulary
Teaching grammar
Teaching phonology
Teaching discourse
Teaching listening
Teaching speaking
Teaching reading
Teaching writing
Assessment principles
Using assessment to inform learning
Classroom language
Language models
Recognizing learner errors
Communicating with other professionals
CEFR level
Language awareness
Terminology for describing language
Reference materials
Classroom observation
Reflecting on teaching and learning
Planning own development
Teacher research
Teamwork and collaboration
Professional roles and responsibilities

Figure 3.12 Summary of the areas of competence covered by the Cambridge English Teaching Framework

One noticeable point of comparison is that the Cambridge English Teaching Framework appears to place greater emphasis on **teaching techniques** and **language proficiency** and awareness, while the British Council CPD Framework pays more attention to broader educational issues, such as knowledge of the subject, inclusiveness, and 21st century skills. This may well be because of the desire of Cambridge English to relate the competences to its teacher training qualifications, preparation for which places emphasis on developing practical classroom skills of the kind developed and promoted in English-speaking countries, and also on the knowledge and understanding related to these skills. In contrast, the British Council CPD Framework takes a broader view of the role of English language teaching in education, including its role in CLIL contexts, which is underpinned by its global mission.

This comparison highlights the ways in which frameworks of competences depend on the mission and values of the organizations or individuals that develop them, as well as the purpose for which each framework is developed. It also highlights the cumulative nature of the development of such frameworks: in the case of both the Cambridge English Teaching Framework and the British Council CPD Framework, various pre-existing frameworks (including the EPG and the Eaquals TD Framework) were referred to, and the approach to describing and laying out descriptors was adapted to suit the purposes of the respective organizations.

Specialized frameworks for teachers

A difficulty with generic frameworks of competences is that they cannot encompass the whole field of education—even though, as can been seen in this chapter, there are many overlaps between specialisms and sectors. In the case of language education, the breadth and diversity spans different specialisms, such as teaching in CLIL contexts, and diverse sectoral requirements, such as those relating to teaching young learners or company employees.

It comes as no surprise, therefore, that a number of frameworks of specialized language teaching competences have been developed. The ECML, who oversaw the development of EPOSTL, were involved in creating the two examples of specialized frameworks described below.

European Framework for CLIL Teacher Education

The CLIL approach has become popular, especially in Europe, as a means of intensifying the development of students' proficiency in the second/foreign language (often English). The idea is that students work on both the subject in question and the additional language at the same time: teachers of certain subjects (or language teachers) are asked to teach some subject lessons each week in the additional language and to support students in the learning of relevant aspects of that language.

The European Framework for CLIL Teacher Education (ECML, 2011; see Website references) is a good example of a framework that is focused on professional development rather than on setting standards. The descriptors of 'target professional competences' in it are linked directly to 'professional development components' (PDCs) in a separate section of the Framework, which together form a framework curriculum for CLIL teacher education (actual resources for development, which would need to be language- and context-specific, are not provided). Each module in the curriculum consists of non-sequential components and a brief description. These descriptions are based on, and link back to, the 'target professional competences'. For example, under the heading 'Learning resources and environments', we find the list shown in Figure 3.13.

CLIL teachers are able:

a) to maintain a triple focus on content, language and learning skills (PDC 4, 5, 8)

b) to design and use cognitively and linguistically appropriate learning materials (PDC 4, 5, 8)

c) to create criteria for developing CLIL resources (including multimedia) that embed the core features of CLIL (PDC 8)

d) to describe criteria and strategies for using non-classroom and non-school learning environments (PDC 5, 11)

e) to assess learning resources and environments and to identify potential difficulties and solutions to overcome these (PDC 4, 8, 11)

f) to articulate techniques for developing co-operative networks aimed at choosing, creating, adapting and accessing materials or developing learning resources and accessing learning environments (PDC 8, 11)

g) to help students build cross-curricular links (PDC 4, 8, 11)

Figure 3.13 Some descriptors from the European Framework for CLIL Teacher Education (ECML, 2011)

Here, the relevant PDCs include those under the heading 'Designing CLIL classroom curricula', as shown in Figure 3.14.

• Theoretical constructs of curriculum design
• CLIL course construction
       Objectives/targets of content learning
       Course syllabus (including learner–teacher negotiation)
       Cross-curricular linkages
       Planned learning outcomes (content, language, learning skills, and cognition)
       Intercultural aspects of course design
       Design of teaching and learning units/modules
• CLIL course scheduling
       Embedding CLIL in the school curriculum
       Time allocation
       Teacher interaction and co-operation
                (Competence standards: 4, 7, 8)

Figure 3.14 Designing CLIL classroom curricula (ECML, 2011, p. 33)

Activity 3.8   If you were an experienced language teacher beginning to work in CLIL, what kinds of professional development support would you need in order to meet the competence requirements outlined in Figure 3.13?

The implications of the competence requirements in Figure 3.13 are considerable. Maintaining a 'triple focus' on content (for example, a biology topic such as photosynthesis), language (for example, making comparisons), and learning skills (for example, deduction) requires a different approach from that which is normally adopted in language teaching. In general language teaching, there is often a dual focus—on, say, an aspect of language and on the content of language teaching materials—or even a triple focus, with an additional focus on ways of handling listening comprehension as a learning skill. However, unlike CLIL students, students in general language courses are not usually expected to learn the subject matter of the units in the textbook, which may be about a variety of topics of general interest, from food to entertainment, history, and personality testing. Similarly, to design and use cognitively and linguistically appropriate learning materials is a competence that requires considerable previous experience under the guidance of more experienced colleagues. In short, even for experienced language teachers, some intensive further training and development is desirable, such as observation of experienced CLIL teachers, reading in the area of CLIL, lesson preparation in co-operation with an experienced CLIL teacher, and so on.

These links between competence standards and indicators of professional development in the CLIL framework are similar to the approach taken in the European Profile discussed on page 25, where the additional quality guidelines are matched with the strategies and skills in the main framework. This is an approach also used by the **British Association of Lecturers in English for Academic Purposes** (**BALEAP**), which is the focus of the next section.

Competency Framework for Teachers of English for Academic Purposes

The Competency Framework for Teachers of English for Academic Purposes (BALEAP, 2008; see Website references) aims to provide a systematic overview of the competences needed by teachers working in the field of **English for Academic Purposes** (**EAP**), primarily in UK academic settings or in settings which are modelled on those in the UK. It begins with a global set of competences relating to four main areas: 'academic practice', 'EAP students', 'curriculum development', and 'programme implementation'. A summary of the competency statements is shown in Figure 3.15.

Academic practice	an EAP teacher will –
Academic contexts	have a reasonable knowledge of the organizational, educational and communicative policies, practices, values and conventions of universities.
Disciplinary differences	be able to recognize and explore disciplinary differences and how they influence the way knowledge is expanded and communicated.
Academic discourse	have a high level of systemic language knowledge including knowledge of discourse analysis.
Personal learning, development and autonomy	recognize the importance of applying to his or her own practice the standards expected of students and other academic staff.
EAP students	**an EAP teacher will understand –**
Student needs	the requirements of the target context that students wish to enter as well as the needs of students in relation to their prior learning experiences and how these might influence their current educational expectations.
Student critical thinking	the role of critical thinking in academic contexts and will employ tasks, processes and interactions that require students to demonstrate critical thinking skills.
Student autonomy	the importance of student autonomy in academic contexts and will employ tasks, processes and interactions that require students to work effectively in groups or independently as appropriate.
Curriculum development	**an EAP teacher will understand –**
Syllabus and programme development	the main types of language syllabus and will be able to transform a syllabus into a programme that addresses students' needs in the academic context within which the EAP course is located.
Text processing and text production	approaches to text classification and discourse analysis and will be able to organize courses, units and tasks around whole texts or text segments in ways that develop students' processing and production of spoken and written texts.
Programme implementation	**an EAP teacher will be –**
Teaching practices	familiar with the methods, practices and techniques of communicative language teaching and be able to locate these within an academic context and relate them to teaching the language and skills required by academic tasks and processes.
Assessment practices	able to assess academic language and skills tasks using formative and summative assessment.

Figure 3.15 Summary of competency statements from the Competency Framework for Teachers of EAP (BALEAP, 2008, p. 3)

Each of the four areas is then expanded to provide detailed descriptors, arranged in three groups: 'knowledge and understanding of', 'ability to', and 'possible indicators' (i.e. the ways in which teachers can demonstrate their 'knowledge and understanding' and 'ability'). As an example, Figure 3.16 shows the expanded view of the 'teaching practices' competency in the 'programme implementation' area from Figure 3.15.

Knowledge & understanding of –	Ability to –	Possible indicators –
the key differences between the content and processes required for teaching and learning in an EAP class compared with a general ELT class a developed repertoire of teaching techniques and the rationale for their appropriate use	plan and deliver a programme of lessons based on a syllabus distinguish between teaching subject content, procedural knowledge (e.g., how to go about doing a task) and language knowledge integrate teaching of academic language and academic study skills in lessons integrate study skills into other skills teaching integrate IT into delivery, to enhance IT skills and reflect academic practices respond flexibly and exploit unplanned learning opportunities effectively	justify lesson plans on the basis of students' needs and syllabus. Evaluate a core textbook for a particular context adapt or create materials and explain the rationale behind these reflect on and respond to observation or student feedback on teaching comment on a revised lesson plan

Figure 3.16 Descriptors for 'teaching practices' from the Competency Framework for Teachers of EAP (BALEAP, 2008, p. 8)

While the first two columns of Figure 3.16 are reminiscent of the subdivisions in the Eaquals TD Framework, the third column is an important innovation since it aims to enable the teachers themselves, and those observing them, to verify whether these elements of knowledge and skills are evident in practice. There are, however, no stages of teacher development in the Competency Framework for Teachers of EAP as there are, for example, in the Cambridge English Teaching Framework ('foundation', 'developing', 'proficient', 'expert'). To address this, BALEAP has produced the Teaching English for Academic Purposes (TEAP) scheme on the basis of the Competency Framework for Teachers of EAP, detailed in its TEAP Scheme: CPD Accreditation Scheme Handbook (2014).

The CPD Accreditation Scheme handbook (see Website references) provides a basis for the accreditation of teachers of EAP via a portfolio system. The scheme offers three levels of accreditation ('Associate Fellow', 'Fellow', and 'Senior Fellow') and, therefore, has a broader scope and more detailed specifications than the original Competency Framework for Teachers of EAP. The scope of the revised Competency Framework for Teachers of EAP is shown in Figure 3.17.

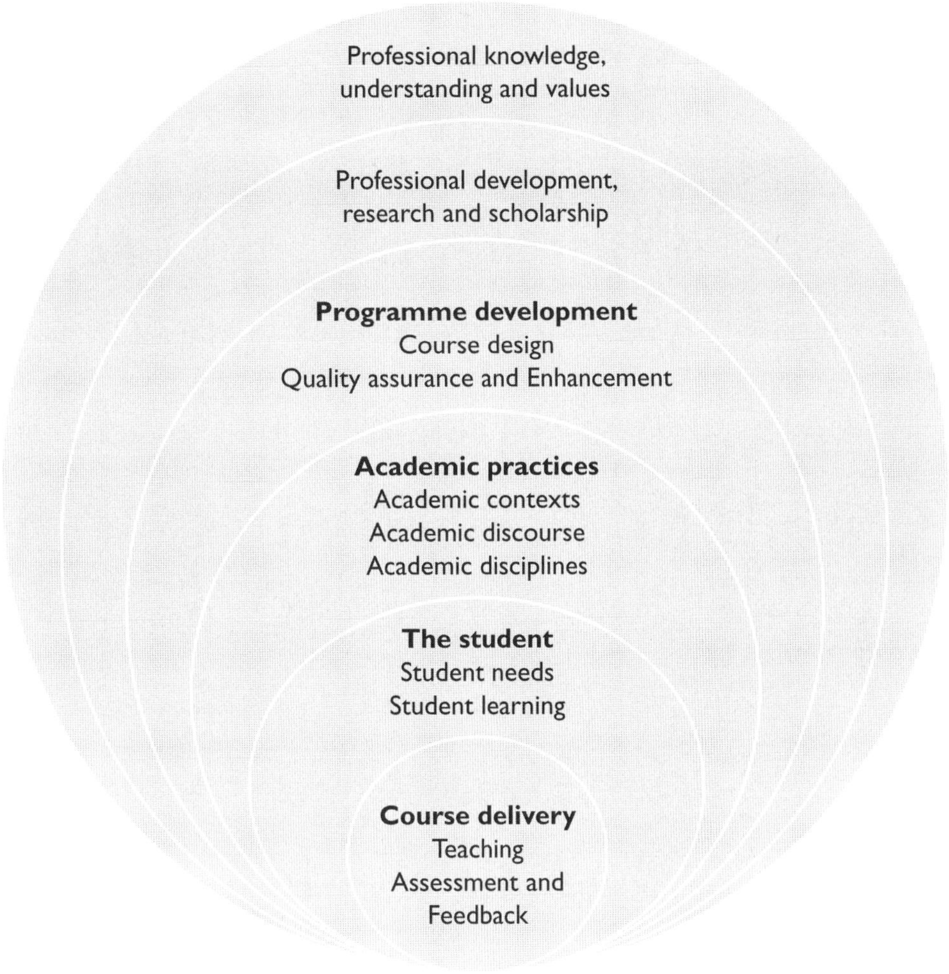

Professional knowledge,
understanding and values

Professional development,
research and scholarship

Programme development
Course design
Quality assurance and Enhancement

Academic practices
Academic contexts
Academic discourse
Academic disciplines

The student
Student needs
Student learning

Course delivery
Teaching
Assessment and
Feedback

Figure 3.17 Scope of the revised Competency Framework for Teachers of EAP underpinning the TEAP Scheme (BALEAP, 2014, p. 8)

A more detailed view of the competences/indicators required for the 'student learning' sub-area in Figure 3.17 is shown in Figure 3.18. The organization is similar to that of Figure 3.15 (see page 45), but the competences/indicators are divided across two levels: one for accreditation as a 'Fellow', and one for a 'Senior Fellow'.

B2. STUDENT LEARNING

An EAP practitioner will understand the relevance of individual differences to practice and the role and importance of critical thinking and autonomy in academic contexts and will employ tasks, processes and interactions that enable students to develop these.

Professional Knowledge & Values: B2	Fellow Area of Activity competence in: B2F	Indicative evidence: B2F
a. the importance and relevance of individual differences in motivation, learning and cognitive styles, preferences and learning strategy use for TEAP professional practice b. the elements of critical thinking and how these underpin academic practice c. critical approaches to knowledge to enable its evaluation and expansion d. the need to acknowledge individual and cultural differences in critical thinking e. the principles of student autonomy f. the pedagogy of supporting student autonomy through group activities and individual tutoring g. the use of new technologies to enhance learning and to support autonomous learning	i. making links between critical thinking and study skills competence explicit for students in teaching ii. providing opportunities and stimulus for critical thinking in sequences of learning activities iii. taking individual and cultural differences in critical thinking into account in teaching iv. making the link between autonomy and academic study explicit to students in syllabus, lesson planning , task or learning resource design v. fostering student autonomy through group activities, one-to-one and through the use of new technology.	i. Observation feedback sheets ii. Lesson plans and rationale Observation feedback sheets iii. Lesson rationales iv. Example documents and statement on exploitation v. Lesson plans and tutorial records New technology use report. Witness statement.
	Senior Fellow Area of Activity competence in: B2SF	Indicative evidence: B2SF
	i. designing courses, materials and assessment tasks aligned with critical thinking and learner autonomy outcomes ii. employing institutional and national level data on the student academic experience to inform practice. iii. leading teams and/or mentoring colleagues in the development of critical thinking skills and autonomy of students.	i. 2 self-produced needs and target situation analysis instruments ii. CPD or management records Team Communication records Witness statement

Figure 3.18 Competences/indicators for 'student learning' (BALEAP, 2014, p.18)

Activity 3.9   Joanna has been a teacher of general English for ten years. Recently she got a job in a university language centre in the UK, where students from abroad take intensive courses in English and other subjects to prepare them to be able to study at degree level in English. She has been advised to use the BALEAP scheme to help her to develop the additional knowledge and skills that she needs for the new job.

Looking at the excerpts from the BALEAP scheme in this section, and comparing them with, for example, the competences described in EPOSTL, what are the main new areas that Joanna will need to become familiar with and competent in? If you were advising her, what practical steps would you suggest she take (in addition to teaching the classes she is given) to help her to develop into the role of an EAP teacher?

If we look at Figure 3.18, where the focus is on 'student learning', it is clear that at least two areas are highlighted which may not have been seen as a priority in Joanna's earlier general English courses: critical thinking and **autonomous learning**. This is not to say that they are not important for students outside the higher education setting; they are in many ways equally important, especially for students at secondary level and above. However, it is the case that they become more important in higher education, especially for students from different backgrounds intending to study at degree level in a language that is not their L1.

Joanna will need to have first-hand knowledge of the needs of these students when they enter degree-level programmes, and these needs will vary from student to student, depending on what they are studying. She could obtain this knowledge by looking at the degree-level course specifications and requirements (how much time is spent in seminars, lectures, and **tutorials**, what kinds of **assignments** have to be completed independently, how assignments and other types of work are assessed, etc.), by talking to tutors about the specific challenges non-native speakers face in the subjects they teach, and also by interviewing some foreign students who are already on degree courses. This should give her a clear picture of the type and amount of autonomous learning that is likely to be required, and the key language skills involved, as well as the difficulties students face when adjusting to this kind of learning situation. Discussion with tutors of other subjects, as well as her own previous experience as a university student, should also give her an idea of what types of critical thinking her students will need to engage in and demonstrate. However, her next challenge is to work out ways of incorporating real opportunities for autonomous learning and critical thinking into her EAP lessons. If she is lucky, the course design and course materials will already include suitable tasks for independent learning that require independent critical thinking that can be evidenced in students' oral and written work. So it is important for Joanna to become very familiar with the EAP course programme and materials and, if necessary, to develop resources and tasks of her own to supplement these. Another step she should take is to observe some lessons given by experienced EAP teachers, and to ask questions and discuss options with these teachers afterwards. It would also be useful if Joanna could arrange to be observed by one of them and to receive feedback.

What BALEAP has done with its scheme, which is aimed mainly at teachers of English in higher education in or from the UK, goes one step further than the CLIL Framework examined earlier in the chapter (see page 42). As well as providing professional development suggestions in later sections (explained in BALEAP, 2014, p. 13), BALEAP offers an accreditation scheme related to the descriptors and indicators in the Framework. The scheme is based mainly on autonomous self-motivated professional learning, as evidenced by individual portfolios. This additional dimension demonstrates the potential of competence frameworks not only to raise teachers' awareness of professional development, but also to underpin professional qualifications and career development.

Finally, it is worth focusing attention on a framework with a different kind of specialized scope that is not primarily aimed at teachers but has considerable implications for their work.

FREPA

A Framework of Reference for Pluralistic Approaches to Languages and Cultures (FREPA) (ECML, 2012; see Website references) is an innovative and complex framework designed to support the development of curricula as well as pedagogy in the area of pluralistic approaches to languages and cultures in education. These are defined as 'didactic approaches which use teaching/learning activities involving several (i.e. more than one) varieties of languages or cultures' (ECML, 2012, p. 6). FREPA thus follows in the footsteps of the **Common European Framework of Reference for Languages** (**CEFR**) and various other **Council of Europe** publications that highlight the importance of such pluralistic approaches and promote them because of the contribution they can make to personal development, intercultural communication, and to the general well-being of society.

According to the introduction (p. 10), FREPA is intended for a cross section of potential users:

- those involved in curriculum development or developing school programmes
- those responsible for the development of teaching materials, whether specifically designed for putting into practice pluralistic approaches or for more 'traditional' teaching
- teachers of languages or other subjects, who reflect on the linguistic dimension of their teaching
- those involved in the training of teachers, whether they already apply pluralistic approaches or not.

In this sense, FREPA is more ambitious than other frameworks referred to in this chapter. The ECML and the authors of FREPA see pluralistic approaches to education as relevant not just to language education but across the curriculum. The descriptors therefore describe the competences needed by anyone, including students, involved in pluralistic education, but they do not focus on pedagogic issues. Another difference between FREPA and other frameworks cited is that the descriptors are linked to specific examples of resources that can be used or adapted to develop the various competences described.

The descriptors in FREPA cover knowledge, skills, and attitudes. For example, the list of descriptors for the 'skills' resource is divided into the following seven sections:

- Can observe/can analyse
- Can recognize/identify
- Can compare
- Can talk about languages and cultures
- Can use what one knows of a language in order to understand another language or to produce in another language
- Can interact
- Knows how to learn.

While the FREPA competences are not distributed over successive phases or stages of development, the list above progresses from less demanding ('Can recognize') to more demanding skills ('Can use'). Figure 3.19 lists the descriptors contained in the first subsection of the 'Can interact' section.

Can interact in situations of contact between languages/cultures

1 Can communicate in bi/plurilingual groups taking into account the repertoire of one's interlocutors
    1.1 Can reformulate (by simplifying the structure of the utterance, by varying the vocabulary and/or by making an effort to pronounce more clearly)
    1.2 Can discuss strategies for interaction
2 Can ask for help when communicating in bi/plurilingual groups
    2.1 Can ask an interlocutor to reformulate what has been said
    2.2 Can ask an interlocutor to repeat what has been said in a simpler way
    2.3 Can ask an interlocutor to switch to another language
3 Can communicate while taking sociolinguistic and/or sociocultural differences into account
    3.1 Can use formulae of politeness appropriately
    3.2 Can use forms of address appropriately
    3.3 Can resort to different speech registers according to the situation
    3.4 Can use metaphoric/idiomatic expressions/formulae in accordance with the cultural background of one's interlocutors
4 Can communicate between languages
    4.1 Can give an account in one language of information encountered in another language/other languages
        4.1.1 Can present a commentary or exposé in one language based on a plurilingual set of documents
5 Can activate bilingual or plurilingual communication in relevant situations
    5.1 Can vary or alternate languages, linguistic codes and/or modes of communication
    5.2 Can produce a text in which registers, varieties, or languages alternate functionally (when the situation allows).

Figure 3.19 Descriptors of 'Can interact' skills listed in one subsection of FREPA (ECML, 2012)

Activity 3.10   Look at the list of descriptors in Figure 3.19. Select the three skills which you consider the most important for students learning a language at intermediate level, and three skills which language teachers should definitely be able to deploy in the classroom.

It can be seen that the language of the descriptors in Figure 3.19 is more complex and, in some ways, more demanding than the descriptors of general teaching competences found in the other frameworks examined in this chapter. Many of the descriptors are relevant to both students and teachers in an educational setting where more than one language is in use and more than one culture is represented. For students, the descriptors in sections 1 and 2 are virtually essential, while those in sections 3 and 4 are important and useful for teachers, depending on the situation.

Conclusion

There are several other frameworks that could have been included in this chapter, but it is already clear from this brief overview of a diverse range of frameworks that many different approaches can be taken depending on the purpose and the target audience of the given framework. In fact, they can all be used for various purposes: as guidance and standards, as instruments for raising awareness through self-assessment and reflection, as a means of assessing where teachers are in their professional development, and as a way of stimulating further development and career progression. It is really up to the organization and individuals promoting the use of a given framework to provide clear guidance to potential users and, above all, to try to ensure that it is not misunderstood or misused. The prospect of using these apparently rigid frameworks may seem daunting to many teachers at first, especially if they are unfamiliar with the concepts and principles underpinning them. It is therefore crucial for anyone or any organization promoting the use of a competence framework by or with teachers to first make sure they fully understand the potential advantages and processes involved.

4

EUROPEAN PROFILING GRID

Introduction

As has been seen in Chapter 3, the EPG is not the first framework of competences related to foreign language teaching. For the precursor to the EPG—the Eaquals Profiling Grid—inspiration was drawn both from the European Profile for Language Teacher Education (Kelly & Grenfell, 2005) and the European Portfolio for Student Teachers of Languages (ECML, 2006; see Website references), as well as from general frameworks such as the AITSL and LLUK examples.

<table>
<tr>
<td>Activity 4.1</td>
<td>

1 How familiar are you with the CEFR for Languages?

  • What are the names of the main reference levels in the CEFR?
  • What three main categories do they cover, and how are they subdivided?
  • Five 'qualitative aspects' of spoken language use are also proposed. What do these cover?

Now check your answers by going to Chapter 3 of the CEFR (see Website references).

2 Has the CEFR featured in your life as a language educator? If so, in what ways have you used it, and how has it benefited your teaching?

</td>
</tr>
</table>

The EPG, available since 2013, is an instrument that describes the main competences of language teachers and presents them in tabular form spanning six phases of development. The EPG is similar to the CEFR in structure and general purpose while being a framework of teaching competences, not learners' language competences. It was partly inspired by the layout and purpose of the self-assessment grid included in the CEFR (Council of Europe, 2001), which has been widely used in language education, most notably in versions of the **European Language Portfolio** (**ELP**) (see Website references).

Like the CEFR and some of the frameworks examined in Chapter 3, the EPG contains a large number of descriptors—most of them in the form of can-do statements (for example, 'can monitor learner performance effectively' or 'can design tasks to meet individual needs as well as course objectives')—and is organized across six progressive phases of development. The key caveats are also similar to those mentioned by the authors of the CEFR:

> We have not set out to tell practitioners what to do, or how to do it. We are raising questions, not answering them. It is not the function of the Common European Framework to lay down the objectives that users should pursue or the methods they should employ.
>
> (Council of Europe, 2001, p. 4)

Nevertheless, the EPG, like the CEFR, does propose a conceptual framework and terminology which should make it easier for teachers, trainers, and managers to communicate about key aspects of language teaching competence and to find common points of reference.

The main purpose of the EPG is to enable language teachers to assess themselves and to reflect on their individual professional development, and also to help managers and teacher trainers assess teachers, which is useful when planning how to deploy teachers and when designing INSET and professional development.

At the time of writing, the EPG is available in the following languages: English, French, German, Spanish, Italian, Turkish, Portuguese, Polish, Bulgarian, Dutch, Georgian, Ukrainian, and Chinese.

Origins of the EPG

The origins of the EPG date back to 2006, when the (now superseded) Eaquals Profiling Grid for Language Teaching Professionals was created by Brian North, one of the authors of the CEFR, and Galya Mateva, a distinguished Bulgarian teacher trainer. The reasons behind it related to the need for Eaquals to inspect language teaching institutions prior to admitting them as members of the Association, and to periodically reinspect them. In most cases, Eaquals inspectors had (and still have) only two days to review all aspects of the institution's work, including, of course, the teaching, qualifications, experience, and competences of the teaching team. Institutions were therefore asked to use the Eaquals Profiling Grid to prepare a **profile** of their teachers for inspectors so that they could more easily access the information they needed, saving time that would otherwise need to have been spent checking numerous teachers' curriculum vitaes (CVs). Eaquals also needed a way of comparing teachers with different qualifications and backgrounds, often coming from a range of countries, and teaching a variety of languages.

Managers of institutions were not always successful in generating a profile of their teaching team, but they did find the Eaquals Profiling Grid useful and, in several cases, began to use it as a tool for teacher self-assessment and development. Following various presentations and workshops outside Eaquals, a consortium was formed to further develop the Eaquals Profiling Grid into a viable EU-wide tool for teacher development. The consortium was led by the Centre International d'Études Pédagogiques in France and consisted of five other main partners (the British Council; Eaquals; the Goethe-Institut; Instituto Cervantes, Spain; and OPTIMA, Bulgaria) and five subsidiary partners (CEBS, Austria; ELS-Bell Education, Poland; Hogeschool van Amsterdam, Netherlands; Sabanci University, Turkey; and Università per Stranieri di Siena, Italy). The consortium successfully applied to the EU for funding to run the project, which lasted two years, from 2011–13.

The main activities during the two years of the EPG project were as follows:

- identifying areas where the then Eaquals Profiling Grid needed development and expansion
- adding new categories and descriptors to create a pilot version of the EPG and translating this into five languages (English, French, German, Italian, and Spanish)
- validating the categories, layout, and descriptors with teachers, trainers, and managers
- using the results of the **validation** process to create a final version
- developing the electronic version, the e-Grid, and the EPG user guide.

The training events that were held in various countries towards the end of the project confirmed the partners' view that the project outcomes were very worthwhile and would be useful across Europe and beyond. Encouraging external recognition came in 2014, when the project was granted a European Language Label (ELL)—an annual award recognizing outstanding projects in language education, sponsored by the European Commission. Since then, seminars, presentations, and workshops have confirmed a widespread need for such a tool, which is now in use in a wide variety of institutions in numerous countries.

Rationale and aims of the EPG project

As described in Chapter 2, teacher development is, primarily, a bottom-up process, and this is the view that was taken by those involved in the EPG project: teachers develop themselves based on the training they participate in, personal career experiences, and their interests. In other words, teachers should see themselves as being mainly responsible for and in control of their own development. Employers for their part have a responsibility to support and foster the development of teachers at the individual and group level through a process of consultation and positive initiatives. Academic managers and trainers, or mentors responsible for providing this support, also have in mind the language centre's need to assure the quality of its courses and to achieve its educational objectives. In this sense, teacher development is a shared responsibility that has an impact on all key stakeholders, including learners, teachers, and employers.

Use of common criteria in the form of descriptors helps to reduce the subjectivity and selectiveness that can arise in the assessment and self-assessment processes. Of course, this is not to suggest that the descriptors in the EPG are the only ones that could be used, but they have been developed taking into account the views and needs of diverse partners in ten different countries and have undergone validation, which is not the case with all such frameworks.

The principles behind the EPG

The following eight key principles underpin not just the work of the EPG project group, but also the prior work done by Eaquals.

1 **An action-oriented approach**. The EPG adopts the CEFR's action-oriented approach to teaching and learning. In the CEFR, the descriptors (in the form of can-do statements) relate to actions that are carried out using language rather than to the knowledge that is needed to carry out those actions. In the EPG, teaching competences are similarly viewed from a positive perspective: the point is not to focus on what teachers are unable to do but what they can do, i.e. the competences they have so far acquired (for example, 'can monitor learner performance effectively').

2 **An incremental approach**. It was important that, rather than proposing descriptors or indicators to fit teachers at the peak of their career, there should be a visible progression from one phase of development to another. Practising language teachers include those at the beginning of their careers without much experience as well as those who have been teaching for many years and have accumulated experience of different contexts and types of courses, and all those in between. The EPG spans six phases of development, and each phase incorporates the features and competences of the preceding ones and builds on them. For example, while at development phase 1.1 there is an indication that teachers are still learning 'the basics', generally speaking at development phase 3.2 (except 'training and qualifications') there are references to helping colleagues with understanding and application.

3 **Modularity**. The EPG is organized according to distinct categories and subcategories. In self-assessment, teachers do not need to cover all subcategories at the same time. They can decide that they will refer to descriptors in only part of the EPG. The EPG is also an open framework. It can be complemented with new categories and descriptors that meet specific needs at the local and national level (very young learners, migrants, languages for university study, etc.).

4 **Self-assessment and assessment**. The EPG is based on the commitment to a culture of self-assessment and self-awareness that is already established in many educational institutions. It is a tool that enables teachers to assess themselves and to compare these self-assessments with assessments carried out by supervisors, trainers, or fellow teachers.

5 **Reflection**. The EPG enables users to think carefully about the results of self-assessment and assessment by others, in order to identify areas for development or change and to formulate a plan of action.

6 **Continuing professional development**. The EPG is intended to be used as an aid for teacher development and to provide guidance for those organizing CPD and INSET for teachers.

7 **Common standards**. The original purpose of the Eaquals Profiling Grid was to provide a framework of international standards for teachers of any additional or foreign language so as to make comparisons easier and more objective, and to facilitate mobility, which is often important for language teachers. The EPG potentially enables institutions or groups of institutions to establish minimum standards for the teachers they employ in terms of teaching competences, qualifications, and professionalism; it also provides a point of reference for the CPD and INSET programmes offered.

8 **The equal value of languages**. Although some languages are more widely taught and learned than others, the principle that all languages are equally valuable is affirmed through the intercultural competences featured in the EPG, and the fact that it is so far available in a growing number of languages and used in institutions which teach more than one language.

Activity 4.2   Put principles 1–8 in order of importance according to the teacher development context(s) that you are most familiar with. Why are the top three that you selected so important for the context(s) in question?

Validation of the EPG

Having consulted widely within the network of EPG partners to develop the descriptors, it was important to validate this work by testing the EPG more widely. This was complicated by the fact that there were five different language versions of the pilot EPG, and that it was necessary to involve not just language teachers but also teacher trainers and managers of teachers in the consultation.

Field-testing with language teachers

The purpose of field-testing with language teachers was to test the validity of the descriptors in the pilot EPG. The aims of this exercise, which was modelled on the process used to validate the key descriptors in the CEFR, were threefold:

- to scale the descriptors (the bullet points in each category of the EPG) to help ensure that they were at the correct development phase, in the right order
- to investigate the stability of interpretation of descriptors across languages, sectors, and so on
- to set 'cut-points' on the scales for the various categories to help to divide them into the six development phases.

This was done by setting up four separate online survey questionnaires, in five different languages. The questionnaires were designed to overlap with each other so that each category of EPG descriptors was covered in at least two separate survey questionnaires. Having provided basic details such as the extent of their teaching experience, the educational sector in which they were working, and the language they were teaching, respondents were asked to assess themselves against four separate categories of pilot EPG descriptors by choosing 'Yes' or 'No'; these were glossed as follows in the survey questionnaires:

No = No, I can't do this. I do not yet have this skill/knowledge.

Yes = Yes, this describes what I can do. I have this skill/knowledge.

Following a publicity campaign by the 11 EPG partners, over 2,000 teachers participated. Valid completed questionnaires totalled 1,818: 705 for the English version, 245 for French, 485 for German, 142 for Italian, and 241 for Spanish. Of these 1,818 teachers:

- around half were native speakers of the language they were teaching
- over 1,000 had ten or more years of language teaching experience
- fewer than 300 had between very little and three years of experience
- the remainder had between four and nine years of experience.

In terms of types of student being taught, numbers were as follows:
- under six years old – 13
- six to twelve years old – 163
- thirteen to sixteen years old – 326
- seventeen to eighteen years old – 205
- above sixteen years old in vocational training, workplace training, or further education – 488
- above eighteen years old in higher education – 622

There were very few differences between the responses from teachers in different sectors of education. The analysis of the results found that 83.2% of EPG descriptors were interpreted in a fully stable manner by teachers across the different contexts, which compared quite well with the CEFR analysis (87.5% stability). Only ten descriptors (7% of the total) had to be eliminated because of unusual or inconsistent interpretation, while several others needed to be retranslated or adjusted. For example, the descriptor 'I have taken part in standardization training for assessing learner performance in terms of the levels of the Common European Framework of Reference (CEFR)' was **calibrated** by teachers as being more difficult than 'I can assess spoken and written proficiency reliably at all levels according to CEFR criteria' which is a logical impossibility. The first of these descriptors was therefore eliminated and replaced. In another case, 'I can evaluate materials from both practical and theoretical perspectives', a quite sophisticated skill, was surprisingly placed by teachers at phase 1.2 instead of 3.1, so this descriptor was eliminated.

Field-testing with managers and teacher trainers

This field-testing exercise was done mainly face-to-face with managers or co-ordinators of language teachers and teacher trainers, or in some cases via email correspondence. Fewer individuals were involved (a total of 100 trainers and 63 managers across the five languages). Specifically, this exercise aimed to:

- find out whether or not the pilot EPG in its five different language versions was perceived as useful for those with managerial or training responsibilities

- test out the organization and sequencing of the pilot EPG in terms of the coverage wording, and grading of the sets of descriptors in the pilot EPG

- gather suggestions and feedback on the EPG as a whole and on the coverage, sequencing, and wording of descriptors

The methodology used involved a combination of the following:

- **jigsaw tasks** in which participants were asked to sort descriptors from different categories of the EPG and order them in the correct sequence according to the phases of development

- assessments of teachers, complemented where possible by these teachers' self-assessment

- interviews with participants about the potential usefulness of the EPG as a whole in their work.

The results of the jigsaw tasks confirmed the weaknesses in some descriptors identified in the field-testing exercise with teachers, while interviews and detailed comments provided valuable feedback that helped to shape the final version of the EPG, and also provided the basis for the accompanying user guide, the online version, the e-Grid, and the various translations that now exist.

Scope of the EPG

As mentioned earlier in this chapter (see 'Rationale and aims of the EPG project' on page 55), the fundamental aim of the EPG is to assist teachers of foreign or additional languages in their development as teachers in order to improve their effectiveness in supporting language learning. The EPG can, however, also be used by managers and co-ordinators who are responsible for assuring the quality of language education, and who are often also trainers and mentors or work alongside trainers and mentors, providing support and CPD or INSET opportunities for language teachers in the institutions where they work. In some cases, they also work with a wider constituency of language teachers, for example in institutions which offer INSET courses to teachers coming from abroad, or with those enrolled on part-time INSET courses.

In order to achieve this aim, the EPG needed to provide a set of criteria in the form of descriptors organized in categories and arranged along an **incremental scale** of development phases. An example of this is shown in Figure 4.1.

Development phase 1		Development phase 2		Development phase 3	
1.1	1.2	2.1	2.2	3.1	3.2
• is learning about different **language learning theories** and methods • when observing more experienced teachers, can understand why they have chosen the techniques and materials they are using	• has basic understanding of different language learning theories and methods • can select new techniques and materials, with advice from colleagues • can identify techniques and materials for different teaching and learning contexts	• is familiar with language learning theories and methods • is familiar with techniques and materials for two or more levels • can evaluate from a practical perspective the suitability of techniques and materials for different teaching contexts • can take into account the needs of particular groups when choosing which methods and techniques to use	• is well acquainted with language learning theories and methods, learning styles and **learning strategies** • can identify the theoretical principles behind teaching techniques and materials • can use appropriately a variety of teaching techniques and activities	• can provide theoretical justification for the **teaching approach** being used and for a very wide range of techniques and materials • can use a very wide range of teaching techniques, activities and materials	• has a detailed knowledge of theories of language teaching and learning and shares it with colleagues • can follow up observation of colleagues with practical, methodologically sound feedback to develop their range of teaching techniques • can select and create appropriate tasks and materials for any level for use by colleagues

Figure 4.1 Descriptors for 'methodology: knowledge and skills' subcategory (EPG Project, 2013)

Activity 4.3	Read the descriptors for 'methodology: knowledge and skills' in Figure 4.1. Find three examples of the differences between related descriptors which indicate a higher and lower development phase.
	Think of a lesson you have observed in a classroom or in a video recording. Referring to Figure 4.1, indicate which phase of development the teacher has reached. Find examples to support your assessment. Do any of the descriptors in the development phase you have chosen *not* apply to this teacher? If so, which one(s)?

Coverage of the EPG

The descriptors that the EPG contains cover the following categories:

1 Training and qualifications

This category enables teachers to consider how their own training and qualifications relate to the suggested standards at different phases of development. It also enables trainers and managers to review teachers' perceived or self-assessed competences against information about their training and qualifications. This category covers the following:

- language proficiency, i.e. proficiency in the target language (the only competence in this category)
- education and training, including university degrees or diplomas, and especially language teaching qualifications
- **assessed teaching**, i.e. teaching practice during initial and further teacher education or training that is observed and assessed, and also teaching done as a qualified teacher which is observed and where feedback is provided
- teaching experience, the accumulated hours of language teaching experience, and the range of different teaching experienced in terms of levels, ages, contexts, etc.

2 Key teaching competences

This category is the heart of the EPG. It covers the following:
- methodology: knowledge and skills
- assessment, which covers the various kinds of testing that teachers are involved in, as well as other forms of assessment
- lesson and course planning, including the aspects of language form and use to be focused on, the activities to be undertaken and the materials to be used
- interaction management and monitoring: the ways in which the teacher and students interact, and students interact with one another (for example, in groups or pairs), as well as the approaches taken by the teacher to monitor students' language and communication.

3 Enabling competences

This category covers competences which support key aspects of a language teacher's work:

- intercultural competence, which enables teachers to work with and establish social and cultural relations with and among diverse groups of students
- **language awareness**, the ability to analyse, select, and model the forms and uses of the target language appropriately for the group of students; this is quite different from language proficiency
- the ability to use **digital media** effectively in teaching and supporting language learning.

4 Professionalism

This category covers aspects which are associated with attitudes to the profession and non-teaching responsibilities, rather than with specific knowledge and skills:

- professional conduct, which focuses on the teacher's willingness to participate in and contribute actively to both their professional development and that of their colleagues
- administration: the ability to deal with administrative tasks effectively and efficiently; and also co-ordination.

Activity 4.4

In your experience, which of the four categories described above receives most attention and least attention in the following contexts?
- initial teacher education or training
- classroom observation with practising teachers
- INSET workshops

Using the e-Grid

Chapters 9 and 10 deal in detail with ways of using the EPG for assessment and self-assessment. Here the focus is on the general practicalities involved.

The e-Grid is a digital version of the EPG (see Website references). It enables users to complete an assessment or a self-assessment online, and thereby generate a profile such as the one shown in Figure 4.2. It has three separate entry points: one for teachers, a second for teacher trainers, and a third for managers. The view of the descriptors is the same in each case: one category appears at a time, and the user selects the most appropriate set of descriptors. The differences are in the details to be provided beforehand and the nature of the resulting profiles.

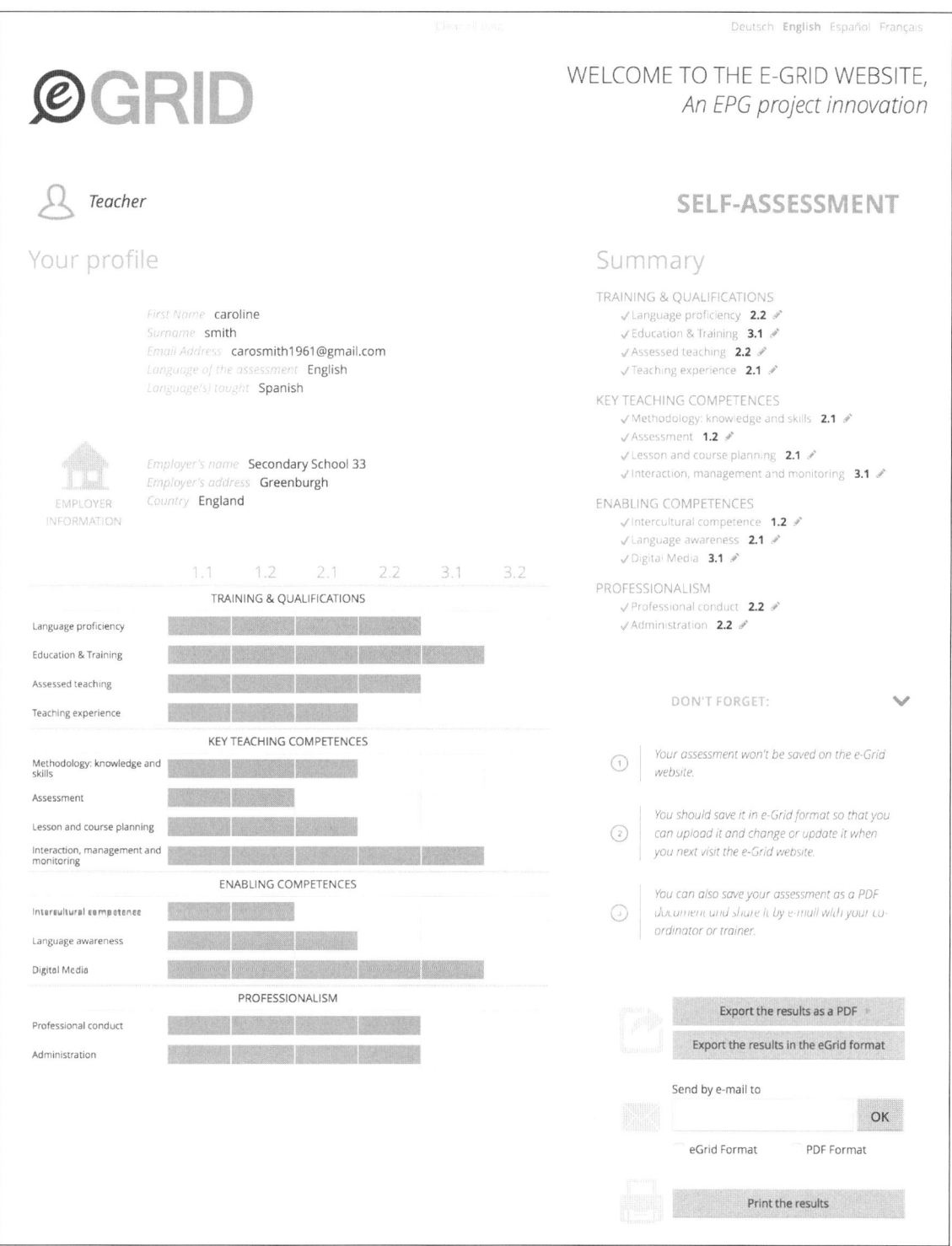

Figure 4.2 Self-assessment by a (fictitious) teacher of Spanish working in the UK

The self-assessment in Figure 4.2 clearly shows the 'profile' of the teacher concerned in graphic form, and also gives a numerical summary. As can be seen in the bottom-right corner, the profile can be saved, emailed, and/or printed. The saved or printed version will include only the graphic summary, with a date at the bottom. This enables the teacher to use the self-assessment, for example in an **appraisal** or a review meeting with a manager. Consider the case below, described by the director of studies of an Eaquals-accredited language centre in the Czech Republic:

> *'Where I find the EPG most useful is as a DOS [director of studies]. I like to have teachers send me their self-assessment and I compare that to the assessment I have made of them. I then discuss any differences with the teacher. It allows me to see if a teacher is being honest with themselves about their professional development. Too often, native speakers [of the target language] over-estimate their abilities; while non-native speakers tend to under-estimate themselves.'*

By saving their profiles in the e-Grid format, teachers can return to the self-assessment at a later date and also share it for amendment and discussion with their trainer or supervisor.

Activity 4.5

If you were the teacher whose profile is shown in Figure 4.2, what actions would you plan in terms of professional development, and what would the actions depend on?

Now, complete your own self-assessment using the EPG. Use either the blank grid in Appendix 1 or the e-Grid online. Then, answer the following questions:

- Which descriptors, if any, do you feel less confident about?
- What did you find hardest about this self-assessment experience? What would make it easier?

The EPG in action

To see how the EPG works in practice in a whole-school context, we can take a language school in France as an example. The school administrators start by creating profiles of teachers and teams of teachers as indicated in Figure 4.3.

This kind of team profile (which can include several more teachers) is useful for identifying where the strengths in a team are. This can be helpful when deciding who should teach which classes, who can help with INSET, and for tracking individual professional development needs.

Jean Dupont		Juliane Henri		Marianne Martin	
TRAINING & QUALIFICATIONS		**TRAINING & QUALIFICATIONS**		**TRAINING & QUALIFICATIONS**	
Language proficiency	1.1	Language proficiency	3.2	Language proficiency	3.2
Education & Training	2.2	Education & Training	3.2	Education & Training	3.2
Assessed teaching	3.2	Assessed teaching	1.1	Assessed teaching	3.1
Teaching experience	1.2	Teaching experience	3.2	Teaching experience	2.2
KEY TEACHING COMPETENCES		**KEY TEACHING COMPETENCES**		**KEY TEACHING COMPETENCES**	
Methodology: knowledge and skills	2.2	Methodology: knowledge and skills	3.1	Methodology: knowledge and skills	3.1
Assessment	3.1	Assessment	1.2	Assessment	2.1
Lesson and course planning	2.2	Lesson and course planning	2.2	Lesson and course planning	1.1
Interaction, management and monitoring	1.1	Interaction, management and monitoring	3.2	Interaction, management and monitoring	3.1
ENABLING COMPETENCES		**ENABLING COMPETENCES**		**ENABLING COMPETENCES**	
Intercultural competence	2.2	Intercultural competence	3.2	Intercultural competence	1.2
Language awareness	2.1	Language awareness	3.2	Language awareness	2.2
Digital Media	3.1	Digital Media	2.1	Digital Media	1.2
PROFESSIONALISM		**PROFESSIONALISM**		**PROFESSIONALISM**	
Professional conduct	2.2	Professional conduct	2.2	Professional conduct	3.1
Administration	1.2	Administration	2.1	Administration	3.2

Figure 4.3 Summary profile of three French teachers showing the differences between them in terms of training, qualifications, and competence (http://egrid.epg-project.eu/)

Activity 4.6   Looking at these profiles, consider the relative strengths and possible weaknesses of the three teachers as members of the same team.

Conclusion

This chapter first outlined the origins of the EPG and the ways in which it took into account some other frameworks of competences for teaching in general, and for language teaching in particular. It went on to discuss the key principles behind the EPG, which include the importance of taking a positive view of teacher development rather than one which focuses on highlighting deficiencies, the key roles that self-assessment and reflection play, and the fact that it is incremental, **modular**, and multilingual in character.

Following a brief account of the steps taken to test out the pilot EPG with teachers, teacher trainers, and managers prior to creating a final version, an overview of the EPG and its contents was provided. The 'methodology: knowledge and skills' subcategory was used as an example to illustrate the EPG's scales of descriptors and how these relate to a teacher's 'phase of development'. The phase of development identified through the process of self-assessment will often correlate with a teacher's length and range of teaching experience. However, this is not always the case: it is possible for teachers with many years of experience to have competences in some areas that are at development phase 1 or 2. Similarly, certain teachers with relatively little experience may assess themselves or be assessed as being at development phase 3 in certain areas. The chapter ended by looking briefly at the online version of the EPG, the e-Grid, and the ways in which this can be used to create a self-assessed and/or manager- or trainer-assessed profile of an individual or a group of teachers.

PART THREE

5 TRAINING AND QUALIFICATIONS

Introduction

The aim of the 'training and qualifications' category of the EPG described in this chapter is to enable language teachers to reflect on relevant aspects of their CV, and to allow employers to review teachers' professional profiles against objective international criteria (in other words, criteria which are not tied to any particular national scheme of teacher education or qualifications). So this chapter is not primarily about teaching competences but rather about the background information on teachers which is essential for an understanding of their current development phase and competence profile. Figure 5.1 summarizes the contents of this category and the rationale behind the subcategories, each of which will be examined in more detail in this chapter.

Subcategory	Rationale
Language proficiency, i.e. proficiency in the target language	Competence in the language being taught is a prerequisite for language teachers. However, the level of competence required varies according to the demands of the teaching context as well as the teacher's background.
Education and training, especially related to language teaching	Quite a few language teachers begin teaching simply because they are native speakers of the target language or have a strong command of it. However, for the purposes of the EPG, it is proposed that specialized teacher education or teacher training leading to a recognized qualification is a requirement for competent teachers.
Assessed teaching, i.e. teaching which has been observed and on which feedback has been given	Theoretical training without practical hands-on classroom experience is not sufficient. Moreover, some of the practical teaching done by teachers during their training and since completing their training needs to have been observed and formally assessed, and feedback on that assessment needs to have been shared with the trainees or teachers.
Teaching experience	Often the length and breadth of a teacher's experience are seen as the main factors to be taken into account for recruitment, performance appraisal, and promotion. However, the EPG proposes that experience should be considered alongside the three other subcategories listed.

Figure 5.1 Subcategories of 'training and qualifications' and the rationale for them

Activity 5.1   In your experience of working as a teacher and/or with teachers, which of the subcategories in Figure 5.1 do you think has the most important impact on teaching competence, and which has the least impact? Does this depend on each individual?

Language proficiency

The subcategory on language proficiency is the only one which relates to competences in this category of the EPG. It underlines the fact that, however little experience or training teachers have, and however seldom their teaching has been assessed, an ability to use the language being taught is essential. It should be noted that, instead of using terms like 'intermediate' or 'advanced'—that may be interpreted differently by different people—the point of reference is the global scale of the CEFR. This is not to imply that the CEFR is the only scale available, simply that it is the most suitable for the purposes of the EPG. Figure 5.2 contains the 11 descriptors of language proficiency.

Development phase 1		Development phase 2		Development phase 3	
1.1	1.2	2.1	2.2	3.1	3.2
• is studying the target language at tertiary level • has achieved B1 proficiency in the target language	• is studying the target language at tertiary level • has achieved B2 proficiency in the target language	• has gained a B2 **examination certificate** in the target language and has oral competence at C1 level	• has gained a C1 examination certificate in the target language OR • has a degree in the target language and proven proficiency at C1 level	• has gained a C2 examination certificate OR • has a degree in the target language and proven proficiency at C2 level	• has a language degree or C2 examination certificate plus a natural command of the target language OR • has native speaker competence in the target language

Figure 5.2 Language proficiency descriptors from the EPG

Activity 5.2   Read through the descriptors in Figure 5.2.

Is there anything about them that surprises you? If so, what?

Do you think it is important for teachers who are not native speakers to have a formal qualification in the language they are teaching? Why/Why not?

In the context in which you work, what CEFR level do you think is the minimum required for all teachers? Why?

Some readers may find it surprising that, according to the EPG, a teacher trainee may have a command of the target language as low as B1, and that even teachers at higher phases of development are not necessarily expected to have a language degree in the target language. It is important to remember that growing numbers of language teachers work with students at pre-primary and early primary level or in other contexts where they are beginning to learn an additional language. Teachers with B1-level language proficiency may not find it easy to teach at a level higher than A1, but it is also true that many teachers with a high level of competence in the target language find elementary levels the most difficult to teach because they need to be able to regulate their own use of the target language and their expectations of students' ability to use it.

In many countries, a university degree in the target language is a common prerequisite for language teachers, at least for those who are non-native speakers. However, there are many teachers who are successful without having studied the language at university, and it is also true that some language degrees do not guarantee that students attain the level of oral proficiency in the target language proposed for development phases 2.2 and above. Furthermore, as was pointed out in Chapter 1, language teachers have all sorts of educational backgrounds and previous professional experiences, including in areas that have little direct relation to language education. Depending on the subjects studied, a degree course may not provide ideal preparation. For example, extensive study of the literature and history of the language, however worthwhile, does not provide the practical experience and insights into the language that teachers working on general language courses need. What language teachers do need is a well-developed awareness of the target language and a proven ability to use it. These may best be demonstrated by having passed a formal examination such as those offered by the examination bodies in the **Association of Language Testers in Europe (ALTE)**. These examination bodies abide by the ALTE code of practice (ALTE, 2010) and apply specific standards to their test development and administration activities.

Activity 5.3	What are the advantages and disadvantages of being a language teacher who is a native speaker of the target language?

Language students tend to believe that it is important for language teachers to be native speakers of the target language and their parents/carers, and other key stakeholders such as the teachers' employers, often share this belief. Commercial language institutions often mainly employ native speakers rather than, or as well as, competent speakers of the target language. In fact, being a native-speaker teacher is not always advantageous, especially if the teacher has not also learned other languages. The possible disadvantages include the following:

- a lack of familiarity with the grammar and pronunciation rules of the target language
- a tendency to misunderstand what students find difficult about the language and to be unable to assist them with these difficulties

- difficulty in selecting examples and materials from sources other than the textbook which are accessible to students
- idiosyncratic use of the language, which may be typical of a given background or regional variety but which may also make learning the language more challenging for students needing easily adaptable models.

There are also some clear advantages:

- an ability to provide good models of native speaker pronunciation, but bearing in mind that there may be considerable differences in the varieties of the target language that native speakers speak
- an ability to spot mistakes or inappropriate use of the language
- an ability to handle teaching at higher levels with confidence
- an ability to make interesting cultural references, even if these are sometimes idiosyncratic or limited to the teacher's own cultural experiences.

It is important to remember that native speaker proficiency in a language does not automatically mean high-level awareness of how the language works and how it can best be selected, modelled, practised, and developed in language classes.

Education and training

Figure 5.3 shows the descriptors used in the EPG of the 'education and training' language teachers receive, both in preparation for teaching and throughout their teaching career. Preparation may take the form of a university degree or a certified course run by a recognized teacher training institution. A major challenge of writing and revising these descriptors was to offer an inclusive view, rather than to indicate a preference for a particular kind of training. Even within Europe, the ways in which language teachers are prepared for teaching and the kinds of qualification they are required to have vary greatly. In some countries, the normal route into language teaching would be via a bachelor's degree plus a master's degree, lasting a total of five years or more. In others, in order to qualify, teachers require a degree and only a single year of postgraduate teacher training leading to a certificate or diploma in education. Moreover, for teachers of English working outside mainstream education, pre-service courses of just 120 hours, often covered in four weeks, are available. In some cases, candidates may not even require a first university degree, or they may hold a degree in any subject, not necessarily related to language education.

As can be seen, looking at international qualifications is complex but necessary. This is especially the case in situations where teachers are employed who have different nationalities and diverse educational backgrounds, and who have taken different routes into language teaching. It is also quite hard to compare very different qualifications without far more detail about the content and requirements of the respective courses. Not all of these various initial teacher education courses will match the criteria detailed in the European Profile described in Chapter 3. Moreover, where specialized courses in language teaching with a practice component

Development phase 1		Development phase 2		Development phase 3	
1.1	1.2	2.1	2.2	3.1	3.2
• is undertaking preliminary training as a language teacher at a teacher training college, university or a private institution offering a recognized language teaching qualification	• has completed part of her/his initial training in language awareness and methodology, enabling her/him to begin teaching the target language, but has not yet gained a qualification	• has gained an initial qualification after successfully completing a minimum of 60 hours of **documented** structured training in teaching the target language, which included supervised teaching practice OR • has completed a number of courses or modules of her/his degree in the target language and/or language teaching pedagogy without yet gaining the degree	• has a degree in the target language with a **language pedagogy** component involving supervised teaching practice OR • has an internationally recognized (minimum 120 hours) **certificate in teaching the target language**	• has a degree or **degree module** in teaching the target language involving supervised teaching practice OR • has an internationally recognized (minimum 120 hours) certificate in teaching the target language • has participated in at least 100 hours of further structured in-service training	• has completed a master's degree or degree module in language pedagogy or applied linguistics, involving supervised teaching practice if this was not part of earlier training OR • has a postgraduate or **professional diploma** in language teaching (min. 200 hours course length) • has had additional training in specialist areas (e.g. teaching the language for specific purposes, testing, teacher training)

Figure 5.3 'Education and training' descriptors in the EPG

are not available (or have only recently become available), a degree in the target language with a theoretical module on language teaching pedagogy may well be the main recognized qualification in a given country. If that is the case, this kind of qualification should not be disregarded by employers in another country.

Activity 5.4	Which of the following topics and elements do you consider to be essential in a pre-service teacher education course for language teachers? Are there any that you think are not necessary at all?

1 Language teaching methodology and techniques
2 Intensive study of the grammar and pronunciation of the target language
3 The main principles and levels of the CEFR
4 Language testing and other kinds of assessment
5 Using digital media in language teaching
6 Psychological aspects of education: motivation, aptitude, individual differences
7 Observation and discussion of live or video-recorded teaching
8 Applied linguistics (the branch of linguistics concerned with practical applications of language studies, for example language teaching, translation, and speech therapy)
9 The cultures of people in different countries who speak the target language
10 The literature of the language
11 General theories of education
12 Using published and online materials

Are there any other topics that you consider essential?

Both the design and content of initial teacher education for any subject, including languages, are very important. However, the reality is that courses leading to the same or similar qualifications are often quite different, even in the same country. The issue of how initial teacher education has contributed to an individual teacher's development is not dealt with directly in the EPG, but self-assessment using the other parts of the EPG will highlight areas where teachers already feel competent, as well as others where they are unsure of themselves.

Activity 5.5	The three people in Figure 5.4 have all applied to work in the same English language teaching institution in South East Asia but have all come into language teaching through different routes. Which of them do you think is, in principle, likely to be best qualified for the job, and why?

Education and training	Angelica	Mark	Liselotte
L1	English and Italian	English	Swedish
Courses on language teaching	60-hour online preparatory course	120-hour preparatory course with teaching practice	None

Bachelor's degree	Art and design	International relations	English language and literature
Postgraduate qualifications	One-year diploma in language teaching with teaching practice	Master's degree in intercultural studies	Two-year master's degree in applied linguistics and English language teaching with teaching practice

Figure 5.4 Example comparison of teachers' qualifications

Assessed teaching

Assessed teaching is a key subcategory of 'qualifications and training'. Many initial teacher education courses include a certain amount of formal assessment of the teaching done by each course participant. However, in other courses leading to the status of 'qualified teacher', teaching practice may only be assessed on one or two occasions, or not assessed by tutors running the course; sometimes there is no formal assessment of teaching practice at all. To make evaluation and comparison as straightforward as possible, the quantity of assessed teaching is expressed in hours in the EPG. This can be seen in Figure 5.5.

There are various ways of assessing teaching through observation. The descriptors here cover at least two kinds:

• Observation of teaching, even a short part of a lesson, in the context of a teacher training course where the trainee and observer are mainly concerned with putting into practice the principles, methods, and techniques which underpin the course curriculum. Some of this observation may take the form of coaching, i.e. providing feedback and advice on specific issues and examples taken from the teaching practice. Other observations, especially towards the end of the course, may be used to assess whether or not the trainee has met the practical classroom teaching requirements of the course.

• Observation of teaching in the workplace by supervisors, trainers, or mentors. Here, the focus is likely to be on quality assurance and professional development. The feedback generally includes a summary of the observer's opinions and practical suggestions for development or improvement.

The key expectations underlying the descriptors for 'assessed teaching' shown in Figure 5.5 are that observers should themselves be (or have been) experienced teachers; that there must be positive feedback on the observation and discussion of that feedback; and that the details (date, length, level, type of course, etc.), as well as the main points arising from the observation and discussion of it, must be documented, for example in a brief report. The teacher should have a copy of the documented feedback, or at least be aware of its content. The topic of observation is discussed in further detail in the companion volume in this series *Language Course Management*.

Development phase 1		Development phase 2		Development phase 3	
1.1	**1.2**	**2.1**	**2.2**	**3.1**	**3.2**
• is gaining experience by teaching parts of lessons and sharing experience with a colleague who is providing feedback	• has had experience of being supervised, observed and positively assessed while teaching individual lessons • has had experience of running teaching activities with small groups of students or fellow trainees (**microteaching**)	• in initial training, has had a total of at least 2 hours of successful documented, assessed teaching practice at at least two levels • in real teaching has been observed and had positive documented feedback on 3 hours of lessons	• in training, has had a total of at least 6 hours of successful documented, assessed teaching practice at at least two levels • in real teaching has been observed and had positive documented feedback on 6 hours of lessons at three or more levels	• has been observed and assessed for at least 10 hours during teaching practice and real teaching at various levels and with different types of learner, and has received positive documented feedback on this	• has been observed and assessed for at least 14 hours during teaching practice and real teaching, and has received documented feedback on this • has been assessed as a mentor or observer of less experienced teachers

Figure 5.5 'Assessed teaching' as described in the EPG

Activity 5.6

If you are or have been a language teacher, make a rough calculation in hours of how much of your teaching has been or was assessed in the ways described on page 74, both during training and as a teacher. How valuable was this assessed teaching in terms of your development as a language teacher?

- If you are a supervisor or trainer who assesses teaching, what kind of procedure do you use prior to the observation, during the observation, and during the follow-up meeting? What form do your records of assessed teaching take?
- How many hours of assessed teaching should, in your opinion, be included in initial teacher education courses? What key criteria should be used in assessing this kind of teaching?

Teaching experience

Assessing teaching experience can be less straightforward than it seems, for two reasons. The first is that many language teachers work part-time and may also be employed for periods of less than a full calendar or academic year. This is especially the case with teachers working on seasonal courses in countries where the target language is spoken. It is also common for teachers to be employed on variable hours contracts whereby the number of working hours varies from week to week, with the teacher informed at the end of each week whether they will work the following week and, if so, for how many hours. This challenging working situation is quite common in contexts where people travel from abroad to attend a language course and decisions are taken at short notice depending on the number of arrivals. For teachers working in the public or state sector, there is also considerable variation. A full-time week in a university language centre may be 12 or 14 hours, while in a secondary school it is more likely to be 20 hours or more. For this reason, the descriptors of teaching experience in the EPG make reference to total hours of experience, rather than to months or years (see Figure 5.6).

Development phase 1		Development phase 2		Development phase 3	
1.1	**1.2**	**2.1**	**2.2**	**3.1**	**3.2**
• has taught some lessons or parts of lessons at one or two levels	• has own class(es) but only experience at one or two levels	• has between 200 and 800 hours documented unassisted teaching experience • has taught classes at several levels	• has between 800 and 2,400 hours documented teaching experience: • at various levels • in more than one teaching and learning context	• has between 2,400 and 4,000 hours of documented teaching experience, including: • at all levels except C2 • in several different teaching and learning contexts	• has at least 6,000 hours documented teaching • has taught in many different teaching and learning contexts • has experience of mentoring/training other teachers

Figure 5.6 Descriptors of 'teaching experience' in the EPG

The second issue is that variety is a key factor in accumulating teaching experience. Indeed, there is a well-known aphorism about teaching that ten years' teaching experience can be ten years of varied teaching or one year repeated ten times. This simple difference can have a very significant impact on teacher versatility and development, and on the level and range of competence attained, which is why the descriptors for teaching experience refer to teaching at more than one level and teaching in different educational contexts (see Figure 5.6). The glossary in the EPG defines 'context' as 'factors in the teaching environment that have an influence on the teaching and the learning process of learners, for example: country, age of the students (primary, secondary, adults), kind of school (public, private), etc.'

| **Activity 5.7** | Consider the following three teachers working in different languages in different countries. Compare their respective teaching experience in terms of breadth and the likely contribution it has made to their development as language teachers. |

Robert (British)	**Socorro (Spanish)**	**Helga (German)**
Private language schools (same organization) in Japan, South Korea, and Taiwan (one academic year in each): 21 hours of classes weekly teaching young adults, teenagers, and young learners – A1 to B2 (total: 2,268 hours) Summer language course centre in England: 20 hours of classes weekly for three weeks teaching young learners and teenagers – A1 to C1 (total: 60 hours) *Total: 2,328 hours*	Secondary school in Ireland: ten hours of classes weekly for one academic year teaching teenagers – A1 to A2 (total: 360 hours) Private lessons for business people in Ireland – mostly one-to-one: three or four hours of classes weekly for one year teaching mixed special purposes courses – around A2 to B1 (total: 100 hours) Language institute in Spain: intensive courses for mixed-ability foreign young adults (A1 to B2) – average of 12 hours of classes weekly for four years (total: 1,440 hours), and summer courses for teenagers – 20 hours of classes weekly plus social activities for four weeks over four years (total: 320 hours) *Total: 2,220 hours*	German mainstream primary school in Brazil: 20 hours of classes weekly for one academic year teaching children learning other subjects in German – A2 to bilingual (total: 720 hours) Private language institute in Argentina: 12 hours weekly for two academic years – beginner to B2 (total: 864 hours) Languages department of a university in Argentina: 10 hours of classes weekly for two years teaching on undergraduate and postgraduate language and literature courses – B1 to C2 (total: 600 hours) *Total: 2,184 hours*

Figure 5.7 Comparison of three teachers and their teaching experience

In terms of the descriptors in Figure 5.6, each of the teachers in Figure 5.7 is at development phase 2.2 of the 'teaching experience' subcategory. However, this is quite difficult to determine accurately without actually interviewing the teachers to find out more about their feelings about the various jobs they have done, their experiences with different kinds of students, and what they learned from their experiences. Each of them has worked abroad, and two of them have done some teaching in their own country. Is such a range of teaching experience enriching? Are there more development opportunities for teachers who move from country to country regularly (like Robert), or for those who stay mainly in the same country (like Socorro)? What are the relative advantages and disadvantages of teaching in private language centres as opposed to working in mainstream schools or universities? These are some of the questions that an employer might want to explore.

Activity 5.8

Use the 'training and qualifications' category of the e-Grid to assess yourself, or a teacher you know well, against the descriptors in this section. In which subcategory does the assessment reveal most strengths, and why? Which is the least strong subcategory?

Conclusion

This chapter has looked in detail at the 'training and qualifications' category of the EPG. The second, third, and fourth subcategories of this category do not in themselves generate a competence profile but rather a factual account, not unlike a CV. Nevertheless, these factors are essential to include in assessment or self-assessment, because what teachers have so far done in each of these areas will have contributed in important ways to the development of the competences covered in the other categories of the EPG. Training and other aspects of teacher education provide a basis on which to build further knowledge, awareness, and skills, and assessed teaching is a vital contributor to the development of competence in the classroom. The challenge for teachers is to use their teaching experience to stimulate their further development.

6

KEY TEACHING COMPETENCES

Introduction

The 'key teaching competences' category covers four interrelated subcategories of competence which are seen as essential in a language teacher's repertoire. These are 'methodology – knowledge and skills', 'assessment of learning', 'lesson and course planning', and 'interaction management and monitoring'. As with other main categories, the order of subcategories is not an indicator of their importance; in all cases, the order could be different. However, it is logical to begin exploring this category with the area of 'methodology: knowledge and skills' (discussed in Chapter 4) to show how the EPG works.

Methodology: knowledge and skills

Methodology has been defined as 'a system of methods used in a particular area of study or activity' (Oxford Dictionaries, see Website references). The 'particular area' that is focused on in the methodology subcategory of the EPG is, of course, language teaching. However, it is worth noting that the methodology of language teaching overlaps considerably with that of any area of education. Indeed, the whole 'key teaching competences' category contains many descriptors which are not restricted to language teaching.

The descriptors in this subcategory cover <u>knowledge</u> and understanding of teaching methods on the one hand, and the <u>skills</u> required to select and use these methods appropriately on the other. Background knowledge of methodology can be gained from talks on and discussion of methodology, or from reading about it during teacher education courses, whereas acquiring the skills necessary to select appropriate methods and use them well comes from training, observation, assessed teaching, and experience. The descriptors indicate that there is a great deal to know and understand about methodology, and that the ability to recognize and use methodology appropriately for different teaching purposes is likely to be acquired gradually throughout a teacher's career.

Activity 6.1	In Figure 6.1, some of the descriptors have been left out. Indicate where each missing descriptor, listed below, belongs in the grid using the numbers provided, and explain why you think they belong there. Then compare your answers to the complete EPG in Appendix 2 (see page 158).

1 can take into account the needs of particular groups when choosing which methods and techniques to use
2 has a detailed knowledge of theories of language teaching and learning and shares it with colleagues
3 can identify the theoretical principles behind teaching techniques and materials
4 can identify techniques and materials for different teaching and learning contexts

You may not have found Activity 6.1 very easy, and it demonstrates the difficulty of finding ways to distinguish between the descriptors at different phases of development. Unlike the training and qualifications category, where qualification types and hours are used as means of measurement, no absolute measures are involved in the 'key competences' category, and this is the case with the remaining sections of the EPG. Instead, there is a gradual development from descriptors which identify basic competence in a given area to those identifying greater competence. For example, in the case of the descriptors concerning knowledge in this subcategory, there is an incremental development from 'is learning about' to 'has a basic understanding of' to 'is familiar with' to 'is well acquainted with' to 'can provide theoretical justification for' and finally to 'has a detailed knowledge of … and can share with others'. Teachers carrying out self-assessment, or those assessing teachers, need to identify which of these best describes their current knowledge and understanding.

Assessment

Assessment of learning is a key part of any language course, and many learners consider it the most important part, depending on their objectives in learning another language. The list below identifies some of the main types of assessment:

- **Placement testing**: to ensure learners are placed in classes and on courses at a level that is appropriate for them
- **Diagnostic assessment**: to identify the specific language learning needs of individual learners (this overlaps with assessment for placement purposes)
- **Progress testing**: to check how learners are progressing after they have completed part of the course, for example after 15 hours
- **Assessing levels of achievement**: to determine what the learners have achieved at the end of a course or a module, and the extent to which this corresponds to the planned learning outcomes
- **Assessing proficiency**: to check whether a learner has reached a given level of proficiency such as B1 or B2, and, in relevant cases, is ready to go on to the next course. Most public language examinations are intended to assess proficiency and can be taken without necessarily having completed a course.

Development phase 1		Development phase 2		Development phase 3	
1.1	1.2	2.1	2.2	3.1	3.2
• is learning about different language learning theories and methods • when observing more experienced teachers, can understand why they have chosen the techniques and materials they are using	• has basic understanding of different language learning theories and methods • can select new techniques and materials, with advice from colleagues • _____	• is familiar with language learning theories and methods • is familiar with techniques and materials for two or more levels • can evaluate from a practical perspective the suitability of techniques and materials for different teaching contexts • _____	• is well acquainted with language learning theories and methods, learning styles and learning strategies • _____ • can use appropriately a variety of teaching techniques and activities	• can provide theoretical justification for the teaching approach being used and for a very wide range of techniques and materials • can use a very wide range of teaching techniques, activities and materials	• _____ • can follow up observation of colleagues with practical, methodologically sound feedback to develop their range of teaching techniques • can select and create appropriate tasks and materials for any level for use by colleagues

Figure 6.1 'Methodology: knowledge and skills' subcategory in the EPG (gap-fill task)

Activity 6.2   What different techniques for assessing language learners do you have experience of? List them and indicate 'which technique would be most suitable for each of the types of assessment mentioned above.

There is a tendency for assessment in education, including language education, to be associated only or mainly with tests or examinations of one kind or another; these usually involve questions or tasks completed on paper or online. But assessment of learning outcomes can and should include a wide range of techniques and activities: paper and online tests, short quizzes, oral tasks that can be done in class, projects and coursework assessed by teachers, and assessment by learners of their own and peers' work, to name just some of the procedures that can be used.

Assessment is an area that is often seen by language teachers as technical and difficult, and it is perhaps for this reason often given somewhat less attention than other topics in teacher education and teacher training courses. The EPG was developed with the view that assessment is a key part of learning and teaching, and that teachers therefore have considerable responsibility in this area.

Figure 6.2 (see page 84) shows the EPG descriptors relating to the 'assessment' subcategory. It can be seen that these descriptors are mainly practical and refer to different kinds of assessment that usually take place in language teaching institutions. Moreover, they cover not just assessment activities but also activities that relate to or follow on from assessment, such as feedback.

Activity 6.3   Anna, an experienced teacher of Spanish, assessed herself against the descriptors in Figure 6.2 and concluded that she was at development phase 2.1. She felt discouraged because she felt she had reached development phase 3 for other key competences.

1 What are the possible reasons for this gap in her development?
2 What steps could she take to develop her competence in this area?
3 What help might she ask for from colleagues and her supervisor?

Lesson and course planning

Teaching is closely related to planning: a lack of good planning at course and/or at lesson level is likely to affect the quality and effectiveness of teaching. This is not to say that improvisation and deviating from a plan will automatically result in a drop in quality; on the contrary, unplanned and unstructured elements in a lesson can add greatly to the dynamic and allow for flexible attention to students' needs and interests.

As can be seen in Figure 6.3 (see page 85), which shows the descriptors for this subcategory, planning involves responding to the needs of students and taking into account how previous lessons have worked out. Even at phase 1.2, we find 'can adjust lesson plans as instructed to take account of learning success and difficulties'. Including 'as instructed' indicates that guidance is likely to be needed at this phase, whereas by phase 2.1, the teacher should be able to independently 'compare learners' needs and refer to these in planning'. By development phase 2.2, the descriptors indicate that teachers should be able not only to plan lessons, but also to plan a course or part of a course on the basis of their analysis of learners' needs.

Activity 6.4

Erika is the academic manager in a language centre where various languages, including English, are taught. One of her more experienced teachers, Josh, has recently completed a self-assessment using the EPG and has assessed himself as being at development phase 3.2 in the 'lesson and course planning' subcategory.

Having observed Josh several times and worked with him for four years, Erika is unsure this is a reasonable self-assessment. What evidence should she ask for and consider in order to assess whether Josh is as competent as he believes he is in this area, and what questions could she ask?

Interaction management and monitoring

This subcategory is about the interaction between teachers and their students. It might be thought that this is an integral part of methodology, but since it is so key to the effectiveness of teaching, it is given as a separate subcategory. It covers three main areas:

- giving students instructions and encouragement so that they can carry out tasks individually, in pairs or groups, or as a whole class
- monitoring what individuals and the whole group are doing and whether the tasks and activities are contributing to learning
- giving feedback to students on the way they are working, and on the language they are using.

Generally, during teaching, being sensitive to the mood, feelings, and needs of students is integral to good interaction management and monitoring. Knowing students individually and how they react to praise, correction, being asked to intervene or to repeat enables teachers to interact productively and to avoid causing upset and unnecessary stress, while at the same time ensuring that all students are involved and motivated.

Activity 6.5

Figure 6.4 (see page 86) contains the descriptors for 'interaction management and monitoring'. Read through them and select one descriptor for each phase of development from phase 1.2 onwards that you think describes the most difficult skill to acquire at that phase.

Before and after observation, what advice would you give to a teacher to help them master each of these skills?

Development phase 1		Development phase 2		Development phase 3	
1.1	1.2	2.1	2.2	3.1	3.2
• can conduct and mark end of unit tests from the course book	• can conduct and mark progress tests (e.g. end of term, end of year) when given the material to do so • can conduct oral tests when given the material to do so • can prepare and conduct appropriate revision activities	• can conduct regular progress tests including an oral component • can identify areas for students to work on from the results of tests and assessment tasks • can give clear feedback on the strengths and weaknesses identified and set priorities for individual work	• can select and conduct regular assessment tasks to verify learners' progress in language and skills areas • can use an agreed **marking system** to identify different types of errors in written work in order to increase learners' language awareness • can prepare for and co-ordinate **placement testing**	• can design materials and tasks for progress assessment (oral and written) • can use video recordings of learners' interactions to help them recognize their strengths and weaknesses • can apply CEFR criteria reliably to assess learners' proficiency in speaking and writing	• can develop assessment tasks for all language skills and language knowledge at any level • can apply CEFR criteria reliably to assess learners' proficiency in speaking and writing at all levels and help less experienced colleagues to do so • can create valid formal tests to determine whether learners have reached a given CEFR level • can run CEFR standardization

Figure 6.2 Descriptors for 'assessment' in the EPG

Development phase 1		Development phase 2		Development phase 3	
1.1	1.2	2.1	2.2	3.1	3.2
• can link a series of activities in a lesson plan, when given materials to do so	• can find activities to supplement those in the textbook • can ensure coherence between lessons by taking account of the outcomes of previous lessons in planning the next • can adjust lesson plans as instructed to take account of learning success and difficulties	• can use a **syllabus** and specified materials to prepare lesson plans that are balanced and meet the needs of the group • can plan phases and timing of lessons with different objectives • can compare learners' needs and refer to these in planning main and supplementary objectives for lessons	• can plan a course or part of a course taking account of the syllabus, the needs of different students and the available materials • can design tasks to exploit the linguistic and communicative potential of materials • can design tasks to meet individual needs as well as course objectives	• can conduct a thorough **needs analysis** and use it to develop a detailed and balanced course plan that includes recycling and revision • can design different tasks based on the same source material for use with learners at different levels • can use analysis of learner difficulties in order to decide on action points for upcoming lessons	• can design specialized courses for different contexts that integrate communicative and linguistic content appropriate to the specialism • can guide colleagues in assessing and taking account of differing individual needs in planning courses and preparing lessons • can take responsibility for reviewing the curriculum and syllabuses for different courses

Figure 6.3 Descriptors for 'lesson and course planning' in the EPG

Development phase 1		Development phase 2		Development phase 3	
1.1	1.2	2.1	2.2	3.1	3.2
• can give clear instructions and organize an activity, with guidance	• can manage teacher–class interaction • can alternate between teaching the whole class and pair or group practice, giving clear instructions • can involve learners in pair and group work based on activities in a course book	• can set up and manage pair and group work efficiently and can bring the class back together • can monitor individual and group activities • can provide clear feedback	• can set up a varied and balanced sequence of class, group and pair work in order to meet the lesson objectives • can organize **task-based learning** • can monitor learner performance effectively • can provide/elicit clear feedback	• can set up task-based learning in which groups carry out different activities at the same time • can monitor individual and group performances accurately & thoroughly • can provide/elicit individual feedback in various ways • can use the monitoring and feedback in designing further activities	• can set up, monitor and provide support to groups and individuals at different levels in the same classroom working on different tasks • can use a wide range of techniques to provide/elicit feedback

Figure 6.4 Descriptors for 'interaction management and monitoring'

Activity 6.6 Assess yourself, or a teacher whom you have observed teaching more than once, using the descriptors in the 'key teaching competences' category of the EPG or e-Grid (see Website references). Which areas are strongest, according to the assessment? Where, in your opinion, is development most needed?

Conclusion

This chapter has been concerned with the category of the EPG that is probably the most important when considering the competences that language teachers must progressively master in order to be effective. This is not to imply that the other sections are not important; rather that they support or enable the key language teaching competences, and complement them.

Each of the subcategories of key teaching competence is itself an amalgam of relevant background knowledge and a variety of skills, as is made clear by the descriptors themselves and the analysis of them in this chapter. It is also important to recognize the fluid nature of the dividing lines between subcategories. For example, there is no way of distinguishing between the 'methodology: skills and knowledge' and the 'interaction management and monitoring' subcategories in 'real' teaching, since using a given method appropriately entails being able to manage classroom interactions effectively. The reason for dividing the competences in the way that has been done in the EPG, and indeed in other competence frameworks, is because, in order for teachers (and others) to be able to reflect on their practice in general, it is necessary to first focus on specific aspects of their teaching and identify areas of strength and areas for further development.

7 ENABLING COMPETENCES

Introduction

As the term makes clear, 'enabling competences' serve to facilitate the key teaching competences. In the EPG, this category spans three key areas: intercultural competences, language awareness, and use of digital media.

Activity 7.1   Which of these three subcategories of enabling competences do you consider most essential in language teaching? Why is it so essential?

Enabling competences alone cannot empower language teachers to teach. However, they are in varying degrees essential when combined with key language teaching competences. For example, in many institutions it is highly desirable to be able to use digital media effectively as part of one's classroom teaching; this may be because these institutions like to be seen as 'cutting edge' and believe that keeping up with technology is a way of adding value to students' learning experiences, so they have often invested heavily in the necessary equipment and resources. To take another example, teachers are not able to plan their classes effectively without a well-developed awareness of how the target language works in terms of its structure, vocabulary, pronunciation, and **usage**—nor are they able to give good feedback, handle correction, or select appropriate examples without this awareness of the language. Intercultural competence is intrinsically important to language teaching, since there is a strong link between a language and the cultures associated with it; and it is especially important in situations where students come from different countries or different ethnic communities.

Intercultural competence

Much has been written about culture in language education and educational curricula, especially in Europe. For example, the Guide for the Development and Implementation of Curricula for Plurilingual and Intercultural Education (Council of Europe, 2010) sets out approaches to curriculum development which aim to develop the plurilingual and intercultural competence of school-age students. Specifically, it focuses on their linguistic, communicative, and intercultural competence as a whole, encompassing the several languages and cultures that they have encountered or may encounter. In the Guide, we find the following definition of intercultural competence:

> Intercultural competence […] makes it easier to understand otherness, to make cognitive and affective connections between past and new experiences of otherness, mediate between members of two (or more) social groups and their cultures, and question the assumptions of one's own cultural group and environment.

(Council of Europe, 2010, p. 8)

A tool developed with the support of the Council of Europe's European Centre for Modern Languages, A Framework of Reference for Pluralistic Approaches to Languages and Cultures (ECML, 2012), which was considered in Chapter 4, detailed descriptors of competences in these areas designed to inform curriculum design and teaching. The EPG does not assume that language teachers will be working in educational contexts where plurilingual and intercultural curricula or approaches are used, however desirable these may be. This is because the EPG aims to provide a resource for teachers of any foreign language in any institutional context. The aim of the intercultural competence subcategory is to first raise language teachers' awareness of the importance of general intercultural competence in their work, and to encourage development in this area (see Figure 7.1). The descriptors cover knowledge and skills related to communicating about and encouraging openness to different cultures in a broad sense. This involves students developing a degree of awareness of cultural differences at the level of history, the arts, gastronomy, social customs, etc., and the ways in which these are reflected in language. More specifically, it involves students understanding differences in culture, opinion, and preferences related to the social and ethnic backgrounds of their classmates.

Activity 7.2

Read the lists of possible dos and don'ts for language teachers below. Choose the two most important in each list, and reflect on why you have chosen these. Are there any you think should be removed from the lists?

Do	Don't
• give presentations and use texts about the culture(s) of the country/countries where the target language is spoken • encourage students to talk about the cultures and traditions of their country/countries • intervene when students criticize each other's political views, religion, or cultural preferences • get students to discuss and think about issues like diversity, prejudice, and tolerance by choosing topics and materials that will stimulate reflection and debate on these issues	• allow students to get involved in discussions about politics or religion • focus on cultural comparisons and differences in the language classroom, or allow students to do so • explain the cultural conventions and social habits of the country/countries where the target language is spoken • choose teaching material which might offend someone in the class

Development phase 1		Development phase 2		Development phase 3	
1.1	1.2	2.1	2.2	3.1	3.2
• understands that the relationship between language and culture is an important factor in language teaching and learning	• is learning about the relevance of cultural issues in teaching • can introduce learners to relevant differences in cultural behaviour and traditions • can create an atmosphere of tolerance and understanding in classes where there is social and cultural diversity	• understands and is able to take account of relevant **stereotypical views** • can use own awareness to expand students' knowledge of relevant cultural behaviour, e.g. politeness, body language, etc. • can recognize the importance of avoiding intercultural problems in the classroom and promotes inclusivity and mutual respect	• can help learners to analyse stereotypical views and prejudices • can integrate into lessons key areas of difference in intercultural behaviour (e.g. politeness, body language, etc.) • can select materials that are well matched to the cultural horizon of learners and yet extends this further using activities appropriate to the group	• can use web searches, projects and presentations to expand own and learners' understanding and appreciation of intercultural issues • can develop learners' ability to analyse and discuss social and cultural similarities and differences • can anticipate and manage effectively areas of intercultural sensitivity	• can use her/his extensive knowledge of intercultural issues when this is appropriate to assist less experienced colleagues • can develop colleagues' ability to deal with cultural issues, suggesting techniques to defuse disagreements and critical incidents if they arise • can create activities, tasks and materials for own and colleagues' use and can seek feedback on these

Figure 7.1 Descriptors of 'intercultural competence' in the EPG

Aside from good interaction management and monitoring (see the section on this subcategory in Chapter 6), which involves being tuned in to the individual needs and learning preferences of students, a different kind of sensitivity is required when dealing with individual beliefs, cultural differences, political views, and musical, artistic, and culinary tastes, etc. It is important for the teacher to be able to establish a climate in the classroom in which each person respects the background and views of others (even while not necessarily agreeing with those views), and where everyone is willing to listen and respond in a way which does not cause offence. They should make sure discussions remain balanced, and indicate clearly when they consider a student's behaviour or views to be offensive, especially if offence is directed at a classmate, or when, for example, racist or sexist views are expressed.

Cultural topics may be challenging, but they can be of considerable personal interest to students and can stimulate authentic interaction in the target language. In a multicultural class, there are excellent opportunities for meaningful exchange and dialogue, and for language learning to broaden students' horizons and deepen their understanding of different cultures.

Language awareness

As discussed in Chapter 5, it is evident that language teachers need a level of proficiency in the target language in order to teach it, although the actual level required depends to an extent on the teaching context, the students' own level of proficiency, and the intended outcomes of the course. But language proficiency does not necessarily go hand in hand with language awareness. Indeed, it is not uncommon for people to have quite limited awareness of many aspects of their own L1, and it has been argued that a language teacher really needs to have learned at least one other language in order to gain a full awareness of their own, and to understand the challenges that their students face.

Activity 7.3	Imagine that you want to begin learning a foreign language of which you have a little knowledge, but you are not yet at A1. You have the option of:
	• choosing a teacher who has learned that language as an additional language and is a native speaker of your language
	• choosing a native speaker of the language you want to learn who also speaks your language as an additional language.
	Which would you instinctively prefer, and why?

The difficulty for teachers who are native speakers of the target language is that they speak and write it instinctively. They have no need to think consciously about grammar or pronunciation; they may sometimes choose words carefully but have no difficulty with vocabulary; and they seldom need to look up the spelling or meaning of words in a dictionary. In these cases, education or training as a teacher needs to put trainees in the position of thinking about their own language from a learner's point of view. Depending on what they studied at school and afterwards, native speakers of the target language may need to learn or relearn basic language-related terminology such as 'verb', 'adjective', 'syllable', 'vowel', 'intonation', and 'synonym' in order to understand how the language works. If they have learned a foreign language, a reasonable amount of their basic understanding of this language will be transferable, especially if it is related to their own. On the other hand, non-native teachers who have learned the target language as an additional language, and possibly studied it in detail to a high level, will probably have no such conceptual difficulties. Moreover, if they can remember what they found easy and challenging about learning the target language, they will be able to anticipate what their own students might find difficult and support them effectively.

Activity 7.4	An awareness of how the target language works is necessary for many aspects of language teaching. Consider what kind of awareness is needed for each of the following teaching situations:

- planning a lesson where the objective is for students to ask each other about past experiences, for example an accident
- dealing with errors relating to the use of prepositions of place (in English 'on', 'in', 'underneath', 'beside', etc.)
- responding to questions about the formal and informal use of words
- helping students to pronounce questions in a clear and intelligible way
- setting up an activity for students to write a letter of complaint
- choosing appropriate material from a textbook to introduce students to and practise language for giving opinions and disagreeing with other people's views.

The necessary awareness or understanding of how the target language works will depend on the language and the students' level of proficiency. However, even with these few examples, it is clear that there is a lot for the teacher to think about, ranging from how the grammar works (for example, for describing past actions) to choosing the right vocabulary (for example, knowing when to use formal and informal language), stress and intonation (for example, pronouncing questions intelligibly), differences between spoken and written language, and the language forms and vocabulary used (for example, to give opinions and disagree with other people). Figure 7.2 shows the descriptors for the subcategory of language awareness.

Development phase 1		Development phase 2		Development phase 3	
1.1	**1.2**	**2.1**	**2.2**	**3.1**	**3.2**
• can use dictionaries and grammar books etc. as **reference sources** • can answer simple questions about language that are frequently asked at levels she/he is teaching	• can give correct **models of language form and usage** adapted to the level of the learners at lower levels • can give answers to language queries that are not necessarily complete but that are appropriate for lower level learners	• can give correct models of language form and usage appropriate for the level concerned, except at advanced levels (C1–2) • can give answers to questions about the target language appropriate for the level concerned, except at advanced levels (C1–2)	• can give correct models of language form and usage, for all levels up except at C2 on almost all occasions • can recognize and understand the language problem that a learner is having • can give answers to questions about the target language that are appropriate for the level concerned except at C2	• can select and give correct models of language form and usage on almost all occasions at all levels • can answer almost all language queries fully and accurately and give clear explanations • can use a range of techniques to guide learners in working out answers to their own language queries and correcting their errors	• can always give full, accurate answers to queries from students about different aspects of language and usage • can explain subtle differences of form, meaning and usage at C1 and C2 levels

Figure 7.2 Descriptors of 'language awareness' in the EPG

The descriptors in Figure 7.2 highlight the crucial role of language awareness in monitoring, dealing with questions about language and communication, and providing suitable feedback, as well as giving good spoken and written models and additional examples of the aspects of language form or use that are being focused on. Providing and eliciting such models play a crucial role in giving students opportunities to repeat and build on them in their own language learning and their communication in the language. Anyone who has recently studied another language will be aware just how important it is to be able to listen to such models, and repeat and extrapolate from them, especially at lower levels.

Activity 7.5   Read through the descriptors in Figure 7.2 carefully. What kinds of tasks and activities would you build into an initial teacher education course for language teachers in order to help them begin to develop this kind of awareness? If there were native speakers of the target language as well as non-native speakers in the group, what impact (if any) would that have on the choice and management of these tasks and activities?

As with most of the other competences covered in the EPG, the most effective ways of developing understanding and the skills needed involve putting trainee teachers in situations (simulated or otherwise) where they need to think carefully about and research the options available to them when actually teaching. An important benefit of this approach is that, through discussion, observation of one another teaching (either live or on video), and reflection, trainees can learn from one another and develop a higher degree of awareness about language and teaching than they could of their own accord. As a language teacher, being able to use a language well is not the same as having a well-developed awareness of that language. One of the reasons that teachers who have been through the process of learning the target language are often better able to provide relevant feedback and guidance to their students and to choose good examples of language in their planning, is that they have become sensitive to the specific areas of challenge and nuance in ways that teachers for whom the target language is their L1 have not. For these native speakers, it is often critical to learn much more about the grammar, vocabulary, pronunciation and use of their own language than they were ever taught at school in order to provide appropriate support to their students—and to continue learning through their own experience of teaching.

Using digital media

It is evident that digital media play an important role in many aspects of life in most parts of the world. In language education, various forms of digital media are seen as providing a desirable, or even an essential, means of extending the range of options in the classroom and enabling students to continue learning beyond the classroom. Clearly, the extent to which digital media are used in language education depends on a number of factors such as the financial resources available to an institution, the educational policies influencing how these resources are used, and the availability of training for teachers in using digital media.

Activity 7.6	How are digital media used in the institution(s) where you work? How easy is it for teachers and students to access the resources and equipment needed to use digital media in the classroom? What proportion of teachers regularly and confidently use digital media in their teaching?

Figure 7.3 shows the range of descriptors relating to competence in using digital media in language teaching. The range is necessarily limited and does not encompass all conceivable technologies; it is likely that it will need to be amended or added to as technology develops. For example, the subcategory at present refers only in passing to the use of **mobile devices**, including those belonging to the students themselves, in the classroom and beyond, even though these present a continually evolving range of teaching and learning opportunities. Given the impossibility of capturing all aspects of digital media, the descriptors focus on what might be seen as basic skills in the field of digital media for education—on skills and know-how that enable teachers to add value and variety to their teaching rather than completely revolutionize it. These include: creating teaching and learning materials using online resources; utilizing basic digital display, audio, and video equipment; downloading and creating audio and video files; and helping less confident colleagues to do these things.

Activity 7.7	Read through the descriptors in Figure 7.3. Bearing in mind your answers to the questions in Activity 7.6, are there any descriptors that you think should be added? What would they refer to? Are any of the descriptors in this subcategory <u>not</u> relevant to your institution; if so, which ones, and why?

Most key teaching competences and enabling competences can be considered applicable, with variations, to almost any language education context. However, where the use of digital media is concerned, the extent to which teachers have opportunities to develop the know-how and skills described will depend to a great extent on what digital media and opportunities for using them are available in their teaching context. If, for example, there is no equipment in the classroom to display digital images, the teacher is unlikely to make use of such images in their lessons. Similarly, if access to the internet is not available in the classroom, the teacher and students will have fewer opportunities to use internet-based resources. Such situations in themselves do not necessarily mean that the language teaching and learning is less effective—or even less varied; it simply means that teachers will have fewer opportunities to develop and use the related competences.

Development phase 1		Development phase 2		Development phase 3	
1.1	1.2	2.1	2.2	3.1	3.2
• can use word-processing software to write a worksheet, following standard conventions • can search for potential teaching material on the internet • can download resources from websites	• can create lessons with downloaded texts, pictures, graphics, etc. • can organize computer files in logically ordered folders	• can use software for handling images, DVDs, and sound files • can use any standard Windows/ Mac software, including media players • can recommend appropriate online materials to students and colleagues • can use a data projector for lessons involving the internet, a DVD, etc.	• can set and supervise online work for learners • can use software for handling images, DVDs, and sound files	• can train students to select and use online exercises appropriate to their individual needs • can edit and adapt sound and video files • can show colleagues how to use new software and hardware • can co-ordinate project work with digital media (using, for example, a camera, the internet, social networks) • can **troubleshoot** most problems with classroom digital equipment	• can train students to use any available classroom digital equipment, including **interactive whiteboards**, their mobiles, tablets, etc. profitably for language learning • can show colleagues how to exploit the teaching potential of available digital equipment and internet-based resources • can design **blended learning** modules using a **learning management system**, e.g. Moodle

Figure 7.3 Descriptors of 'digital media' in the EPG

Activity 7.8   Assess yourself or a teacher you have observed teaching more than once, using the
whole enabling competences section of the EPG. Looking at the results of the assessment
(or self-assessment), where do you consider there is room for further development?
In each case, what activities or training do you think are most likely to lead to that
development?

Conclusion

This chapter has explored the descriptors of the 'enabling competences' category
that support, and are essential to, effective application of the 'key teaching
competences' category discussed in Chapter 6. Enabling competences are no less
important than those key teaching competences, but they are different and in some
respects more transversal in nature. Indeed, these three enabling competences—
intercultural competence, language awareness, and the use of digital media—are
essential in many professions. The degree of importance that they hold in each case
will depend on the context and nature of the job.

8 PROFESSIONALISM

Introduction

The final category of the EPG deals with the important and complex relationship between teachers, their employers, their colleagues, and, potentially, the wider community which the institution serves.

The social status of the teaching profession varies widely from one national context to another. This status appears to depend partly on the extent to which teachers are trusted to do their work and are respected for their collective effectiveness as educators. In some countries, school managers and teachers are given considerable independence and authority in matching the education they provide to the needs of the students and the community they belong to. In other countries, schools and teachers are under a great deal of centralized supervision, and work to detailed national curricula and stringent guidelines. In Scandinavian countries, for example, school teachers generally appear to have a higher status, including better employment conditions, than those in the UK or France, and this seems to relate to the trust that the government and the general public have in them. However, it may also relate to the fact that the educational traditions of Scandinavian countries are different and their populations smaller.

Where language education is concerned, depending on the priority given to language education, language teachers working in the mainstream school and higher education context may feel that they have lower status than teachers of core curriculum subjects such as maths, science, or the main language of the country. For language teachers working in the independent sector, such as private language schools and colleges, or in the corporate sector, the question of professional status is even more complex. Many of them are part-time and, depending on local legislation, several may be freelance and working in a precarious employment situation or have commitments to more than one employer.

Activity 8.1	In the country where you work, think about how the status, terms and conditions, and career opportunities of language teachers compare with the status of teachers in state sector schools, in higher education, and in private schools and colleges (especially language schools and institutes). If there are differences, what, in your opinion, are the main reasons for these differences?

The term 'professionalism' is used in a specific sense in the EPG: it is not used in contrast to amateurism (as in sport) or related to whether a teacher is qualified for a job or not. Rather, it is used to encompass those essential elements of competence, attitude, and values outlined in Chapter 2. Being professional means never engaging in unprofessional behaviour; and, more positively, it implies showing commitment to a profession, in this case teaching, and a willingness to perform professional duties as well as possible.

Activity 8.2

Think of examples of behaviour that, for a language teacher, you would consider to be unprofessional. Assuming managers are made aware of them, what steps (if any) do you think they should take to deal with such behaviour?

Teachers' terms and conditions of employment often cover the most basic standards of professionalism—for example, arriving at work and in the classroom punctually and well prepared, and behaving politely with colleagues and students. Other types of professional behaviour are covered by legislation—for example, sexual harassment, infringement of copyright, and theft of property (such as books and stationery); these are often covered in employment contracts under the heading of misconduct. There are other less obvious areas where teachers can demonstrate their commitment and professional conduct, or may not consistently do so, and some of these are covered in the 'professional conduct' subcategory of the EPG.

Activity 8.3

Which of the following do you consider to be the most important and valuable indicators of professionalism in teachers? Rank them in order of importance (1 = most important), and reflect on the reasons for your choices.
- being willing to work collaboratively with colleagues
- participating actively in the institution and supporting it
- being polite and approachable
- requesting and being open to feedback on their teaching and other work
- taking part in CPD and INSET events organized by the institution
- being willing and able to help colleagues when they need assistance

Professional conduct

Figure 8.1 shows the descriptors for professional conduct, and many of them relate to the issues listed in Activity 8.3. As with all the descriptors in the EPG, the emphasis is on the positive—on what teachers can do and the qualities they have at each phase of development—rather than on what they cannot or will not do, or the qualities they lack.

Development phase 1		Development phase 2		Development phase 3	
1.1	**1.2**	**2.1**	**2.2**	**3.1**	**3.2**
• seeks feedback on her/his teaching practice and other work • seeks advice from colleagues and handbooks	• acts in accordance with the mission and regulations of the institution • liaises with other teachers about students and lesson preparation • acts on trainers' feedback after lesson observation	• welcomes opportunities to share class teaching (**team-teach**) with colleagues at one or two levels • acts on feedback from colleagues who observe her/his teaching • contributes to the institution's development and good management and reacts positively to changes and challenges in the institution	• welcomes opportunities to be observed by managers and colleagues and receive feedback on teaching • prepares for and participates actively in professional development activities • actively participates in the development of the institution and its educational and administrative systems	• acts as mentor to less experienced colleagues • leads training sessions with support from a colleague or when given material to use • observes colleagues and provides useful feedback when the opportunity arises • takes responsibility for certain projects related to the development of the institution	• creates training modules for less experienced teachers • runs teacher development programmes • observes and assesses colleagues who are teaching at all levels • organizes opportunities for colleagues to observe one another

Figure 8.1 Descriptors of 'professional conduct' in the EPG

The main focus in the 'professional conduct' subcategory is on relationships with colleagues, openness to support and co-operation, and participation in the CPD and INSET activities provided by the institution. These are areas that teachers themselves may not often think about, or may have mixed feelings about, especially if they take the view that they are employed and paid only to teach, not to get involved in other activities within the institution. Many teachers are also not keen on being observed and may feel defensive about feedback. One of the dilemmas of teaching is that most of it is done behind closed doors. The classroom may be full of students, but professionally teachers often work in isolation, especially if there is little time between lessons or they have to rush to another location, and if there is no space where teachers can gather to prepare for lessons or relax. More frequently, however, the attitude of teachers to their professional environment and their colleagues is closely related to the way in which they are treated by their managers and those who observe their teaching, and to whether or not the institution takes concrete and regular steps to promote collegiality and consultation on decisions, and offers good support in the form of CPD and INSET opportunities. These aspects of the relationship between teachers and those who manage and supervise them are dealt with in more detail in the companion volume in this series *Language Course Management*.

Administration

Teaching inevitably involves various kinds of administration. Administrative tasks, such as recording attendance, marking tests and other assignments, noting down what was covered in lessons just taught, and so on, are often regarded as a nuisance or a disagreeable chore by teachers. Nevertheless, these tasks form part of their professional commitment and are often crucial for the smooth running of the institution; they may also have important implications for their students. Carrying them out in a timely and professional manner is thus an integral part of professionalism. This is why descriptors relating to administration constitute their own subcategory in the EPG (see Figure 8.2).

Activity 8.4   In your experience, which of the administrative tasks in Figure 8.2 is most time-consuming and cumbersome from a teacher's point of view? Where are teachers most likely to have weaknesses?

However time-consuming administrative tasks can feel to teachers, many are essential to the good running of educational institutions and good teamwork: good administration is critical to maintain good communication and to facilitate collaboration among colleagues. One only needs to think of what happens when substitution is needed for a colleague who is suddenly absent due to illness: if there is no coherent record of what happened in recent lessons, especially the last, continuity can be lost and time wasted. Good administration can, however,

Development phase 1		Development phase 2		Development phase 3	
1.1	1.2	2.1	2.2	3.1	3.2
• completes routine tasks like taking the attendance register, giving out/collecting/returning materials	• delivers required plans and records of lessons correctly completed and on time • marks homework and tests efficiently	• handles marking and report writing efficiently • keeps clear, well-organized records of lessons • hands in documents and feedback by time requested	• handles administrative tasks around the job efficiently • anticipates regular but less frequent tasks and completes them in good time • deals with students' issues, enquiries, feedback appropriately	• co-ordinates administrative tasks with others; collates information, reports, opinions, etc. if asked to do so • takes responsibility for certain administrative tasks such as organizing teachers' meetings, gathering, analysing and reporting on end of course feedback, etc.	• acts as **course co-ordinator** if asked to do so • liaises with the enrolment department, the finance department, sponsors, parents, etc. as necessary • contributes actively to the design or review of administrative systems

Figure 8.2 Descriptors for administration in the EPG

also improve teachers' own well-being because it helps them keep on top of their workload, for example the homework that they need to check or the assessments of individual students' work that they need to record, and can enable them to prepare for lessons more efficiently and effectively.

Activity 8.5	The academic manager of a language centre in Ireland has been assessing her four permanent, full-time teachers whom she has worked with for between two and seven years. She is feeling particularly concerned about the areas of professionalism and administration because a busier season is approaching when a number of temporary, part-time teachers will be taken on, so she wants to improve team-working and efficiency in the centre in order to ensure that everything continues to run as smoothly as possible.

Below are the results of her assessment. What action (if any) could or should she take in each case and collectively?

	Luke	**Siobhan**	**Nuala**	**Patrick**
Professional conduct	3.1	1.1	2.2	2.1
Administration	1.2	3.2	1.1	3.1
Notes	Good team player, but doesn't keep records carefully – lots of chasing needed	Seems not to want to participate much because she is so experienced; quite private, but very efficient	Good to have around, but so disorganized	Has a complicated life outside work, but is trying to show willingness to co-operate

Figure 8.3 Comparison of four teachers' assessments in professional conduct and administration

There is no doubt that these two areas—professional conduct and administration—are quite difficult to handle from a manager's point of view because they are usually tied up with general attitude or personal habits, and certain aspects of these areas are considered non-essential or beyond their remit by some teachers. It is therefore important that the management team makes clear exactly what is expected, and is ready to listen to and deal with questions and suggestions that teachers might have.

Any of the competences in the EPG may be focused on in review meetings during the course of a teacher's career. However, as the competences covered in the 'professionalism' category are not usually focused on in lesson observation and feedback (unlike those in the 'key teaching competences' and 'enabling competences' categories), it is especially important that they are considered in these review meetings. In Chapter 9, ways of combining self-assessment and manager assessment based on the EPG, especially in preparation for one-to-one meetings with teachers, will be looked at in detail. The handling of review and appraisal meetings is covered in the companion volume in this series *Language Course Management*.

Activity 8.6   Assess yourself or a teacher you know well using the entire 'professionalism' category of the EPG. Looking at the results of the self-assessment or assessment, can you identify any areas where there is room for further development? In each case, what steps are most likely to lead to that development?

Conclusion

In this chapter, the focus has been on aspects of teaching that may be peripheral to the central sphere of teaching competences but directly contribute, in important ways, to the ability of an institution to provide quality language education, and indirectly to the well-being of students, teachers, and those with managerial responsibilities. Both in the area of professional conduct and in that of administration, there is likely to be a need to link the EPG descriptors to specific professional opportunities and administrative duties which are relevant to the institutional context, and to what it offers in the areas of CPD, INSET, and collaborative projects.

PART FOUR

9 GUIDANCE ON USING THE EPG: LANGUAGE TEACHERS

Introduction

In Part 3, we looked in detail at the categories and descriptors of language teaching competences in the EPG. In Chapters 9 and 10, we will consider the various ways in which the EPG and its online version, the e-Grid, can be used by the various stakeholders in language education—in particular, language teachers themselves, those involved in language teacher training, and those who supervise and manage language teachers.

As was stated in Chapter 4, whoever the users may be, the main purpose of the EPG is to assist and provide a reference point for language teacher development. It might be felt, especially by those employing teachers, that the EPG also provides a means of managing teachers' performance and career progression. While accepting that the EPG can contribute to performance management and even the recruitment of language teachers, it must be emphasized that it can only serve as an aid to processes that are designed for those purposes.

This chapter will look at various ways in which teachers can use the EPG either by themselves or together with colleagues. Chapter 10 will then consider ways in which teacher trainers, mentors, managers, or supervisors of teachers might wish to use it in collaboration with the teachers they work with.

The EPG and teacher development

Activity 9.1	If you are or were a language teacher, which three of the following had the greatest impact on your own development? Comment on why they have been so important:

- being observed and receiving feedback
- CPD and INSET workshops and other events
- observing other teachers
- discussions with and advice from colleagues
- teaching new kinds of courses
- regular reflection and self-assessment
- other activities and experiences (which?).

If you are a manager or supervisor of language teachers, consider which of the above has the greatest impact on the development of the whole team of teachers you work with.

The EPG is based on the view that, while all the activities and experiences mentioned in Activity 9.1 contribute in different ways to teacher development, depending on the specific background and circumstances of individual teachers, self-assessment and regular reflection on one's work are especially powerful catalysts for further development, especially when combined with these activities and experiences. The terms reflection and self-assessment were discussed in Chapter 2, but both can take many different forms. In this chapter, the focus is on using the categories and descriptors of the EPG when thinking as objectively as possible about one's capabilities as a teacher. The following questions need to be considered:

- What are the practical benefits of self-assessment?
- How often should self-assessment be done?
- What kinds of reflection aid self-assessment?
- What process of self-assessment should be used, how accurately should one try to assess oneself, and what record should be kept?
- Who should the results of self-assessment be shared with? For what purposes?

Practical benefits of self-assessment

The main benefit of self-assessment is a greater and more refined awareness of where one is in one's development as a language teacher. Self-assessment is effectively an opportunity to take stock in a structured manner of one's accumulated knowledge and understanding, as well as one's practical skills, behaviour, and practices in a structured manner.

Of course, although it has been worked on by professionals for a decade and its descriptors have been methodically validated, the EPG only provides one broad set of criteria against which to assess oneself; it is not intended to be used as a tool for assessing fine differences in competence (for such a tool, see the Eaquals TD Framework in Chapter 11). Nevertheless, it has proved to be effective as a general self-assessment tool that encourages serious thought and reflection about what stage one has reached in the various areas covered, and what one needs to do to further develop one's competence.

It is important to note that the categories of the EPG do not all require the same level and frequency of attention. For instance, the training and qualifications category may need reviewing from time to time, especially when teachers are at an early stage in their careers. On the other hand, self-assessment against the descriptors for the key teaching competences and enabling competences is best done regularly, at least once a year, regardless of whether teachers choose to focus on all of the descriptors at the same time, or on just a selection. Doing this will generate an overall picture or profile that can be used to help teachers to decide where their priorities for further development lie.

The user guide that accompanies the EPG includes a series of scenarios which highlight some different possible objectives a teacher might have for using the EPG at various stages of their career. Some of these scenarios are expanded on and developed below.

1 Getting the right qualification and accumulating assessed teaching experience

Having worked as a receptionist in the UK for two years, Gosia has an excellent command of English. She recently had the opportunity to make use of this by teaching English part-time at a language centre in Poland. But she has no formal English language certificate or teaching qualification. Now that she has decided to make a career of English language teaching, she needs to get some relevant qualifications. She looks carefully at the education and training and assessed teaching subcategories of the EPG and realizes that, as well as getting a formal language qualification at C1 level, she also needs to complete a 120-hour teacher education course which includes at least six hours of assessed teaching practice. She registers for an international examination at C1 level and enrols on a preparation course. She also applies to do an intensive course leading to the Cambridge English CELTA, which will give her the opportunity to add to her basic knowledge and skills as a teacher and enhance her CV. In the meantime, as an inexperienced teacher, Gosia realizes that it would also be good to get her supervisor to observe her teaching and give feedback.

Activity 9.2	What other steps could Gosia take to prepare for her teacher education course and to maintain and broaden her English language skills ahead of taking the C1-level exam?

2 Becoming aware of specific needs

Giorgio is a recently qualified teacher of Italian in Italy. He finds some of his lessons quite difficult and realizes that he needs to further expand his knowledge of language learning theories and methods, learning styles and strategies, and his classroom skills in these areas. He refers to the descriptors in the 'methodology: knowledge and skills' subcategory, and also those for 'interaction management and monitoring', and assesses where he currently stands in order to identify some of the gaps in his knowledge and skills in these areas. He then considers ways of making progress. He does further reading on language teaching methodology, and asks his supervisor to observe one or two of his lessons when he is trying out new approaches. He also looks for opportunities for INSET, to help him progress to development phase 2.2 in the specific areas he has identified as requiring further development.

| **Activity 9.3** | What other steps could Giorgio take to broaden his knowledge of language teaching methodology and gain additional skills and techniques to use in the classroom? |

3 Acquiring new skills

Anne-Marie is an experienced teacher who normally teaches French to monolingual, monocultural groups in a German-speaking canton of Switzerland. For the first time this year, she has taken on a fixed-term summer position in France where she will be teaching French to multilingual groups of adults, and she realizes that she needs to develop her intercultural competence. She assesses herself against the descriptors in the relevant subcategory of the EPG, and this makes her aware of some of the knowledge and skills she needs in this area. Before the summer course begins, she does some reading on the subject of intercultural competence and prepares some classroom activities to expand her own and her more advanced Swiss learners' understanding of intercultural issues. She has the opportunity to video-record some of these lessons and to discuss the effectiveness of her teaching with an academic manager. Some of her lesson plans include discussion of social and cultural similarities and differences, and give her experience in handling the special situations that can arise among students from different backgrounds and cultures, and in anticipating and managing effectively areas of intercultural sensitivity.

| **Activity 9.4** | In your view, what kinds of knowledge and skills implied by the descriptors for intercultural competence is Anne-Marie likely to find most difficult as she starts teaching plurilingual and multicultural groups for the first time? |

Michel is a colleague of Anne-Marie's in Switzerland who has been teaching for more than 20 years. He is a specialist in French literature and has so far resisted suggestions that he should use digital media in his teaching, although some interactive whiteboards have been installed in the college. In fact, he only has a smartphone, which he uses for phone calls and text messages. Following peer observation with a younger and less experienced colleague who is quite an expert in the use of digital media, Michel decides that he has to make an effort in this area. He goes through the descriptors in the 'digital media' subcategory of the EPG with the colleague he has observed in order to identify some of the basic skills that he should focus on developing first, and with her help learns how to use a laptop to project images, and to play audio and video clips in the classroom. He then asks the institute to provide support as he gains new skills and more experience of using digital media for language teaching.

| **Activity 9.5** | What other forms of support do you think the institute could and should offer Michel in this area? In the early stages, what is he likely to have most difficulty with? |

4 Growing professionally

Dagmar is an experienced teacher of English. She is familiar with the EPG and has assessed herself three or four times over the last two years. She is also quite ambitious and feels prepared to progress to development phase 3.2 in almost all areas, and, she hopes, become a teacher trainer. Later, she may study for a master's degree in language teaching and applied linguistics or a recognized professional diploma. The area she now wants to concentrate on is professionalism: she is quite independent and has perhaps not participated actively enough in the life of the language centre where she works. She will now ask to be actively involved in organizing INSET events and to take on the responsibility of running teacher development workshops of her own, and will try to participate more actively in other aspects of life at the institution.

Activity 9.6

In order to convince the management team that she is ready to begin preparing to become a teacher trainer and all that this implies, Dagmar could do several other things which are included in the 'professional conduct' subcategory of the EPG. Which should be her priorities?

The main priority for anyone in Dagmar's position—or indeed anyone who is committed to a long-term career in language teaching—is, quite simply, participation. It is tempting for teachers, most of whom work alone in their classrooms day in, day out, to focus on their individual priorities related to planning lessons, preparing materials, marking students' work, etc. However, participating as fully as possible in the life of the institution(s) where a teacher works is vitally important. This is captured by two descriptors at development phase 2.2 in the 'professional conduct' subcategory of the EPG:

- prepares for and participates actively in professional development activities
- actively participates in the development of the institution and its educational and administrative systems.

The first of these descriptors should not be taken to mean it is necessary to participate in every professional development activity; rather, it means participating willingly and positively in those which are relevant—and possibly proposing or initiating others of personal interest. In Dagmar's case, she could consider creating a small reading group to come together on a monthly basis to share views on articles about teacher training methods and principles, or to watch two or three video recordings of teacher trainers in action.

Similarly, the second descriptor does not require teachers to agree unconditionally with the institution's developments and policies, but rather to engage constructively in discussions and projects that aim to help the institution group or improve systems and procedures which are already in place. In relation to their engagement with their manager and colleagues, teachers can ask themselves the following questions: How can I contribute to making things even better from everyone's point of view, including those of the students? What ideas and skills can I offer to the collective effort? Of course, this presupposes managers adopt an approach which encourages, makes space for, and responds positively to, such engagement—this is explored in more detail in the companion volume in this series *Language Course Management*.

Depending on the teacher, there may also be other benefits of regularly engaging in self-assessment. One is that reviewing descriptors like those in the EPG raises awareness not just of one's level of competence in familiar areas, but also sheds light on a whole range of competences relevant to language teaching which one may not have been aware of. This may also help teachers to decide where they want to go next in their careers, and whether there are areas in which they want to specialize.

Frequency of self-assessment

How frequently teachers engage in self-assessment depends on several factors:

- Does the institution where a teacher works encourage or require self-assessment as part of their policy on professional development? If so, it is likely that the frequency as well as the scope of self-assessment will be specified in the policy. For example, an employer might ask teachers to assess themselves against the descriptors in specific sections of the EPG shortly before their annual review meeting with their manager.

- Does the institution offer and recommend targeted observation? If so, the person carrying out the observation might ask teachers to assess themselves before the observation against the descriptors in one subcategory of the EPG—for example, 'interaction management and monitoring' or 'language awareness'—and to share this self-assessment in a discussion with the observer before or after the observation. After receiving feedback, teachers may want to amend their self-assessment in one way or another.

- How much time does the teacher have, and how do they like to approach self-assessment? Time should not be an issue because, even including the time it takes to read through all the descriptors in each category, self-assessment does not take very long—perhaps 30 minutes on average. Besides, as has already been mentioned earlier in this chapter, self-assessment can be done one category or subcategory at a time if teachers prefer, or if time is limited. In fact, there may be advantages in taking an incremental approach to the process because this would allow teachers to focus more narrowly on one area at a time.

However the self-assessment is carried out, it is probably best not to ponder too long or agonize over decisions: the objective is to aid one's development as a language teacher, not to pass some kind of exacting test or engage in soul-searching. Self-assessment is not an exact science, and initial thoughts may actually be more reliable and useful than decisions reached after lengthy reflection.

Activity 9.7	What advice on self-assessment using the EPG would you give the following teachers?
	Elizabeth is a relatively inexperienced teacher. She has just started teaching English at a new language centre. During her induction, she was told about the EPG. Her

supervisor also offered to observe her up to three times in the first three weeks, telling her she should choose which lessons should be observed and what the focus of each observation should be.

Antoine, a teacher of French, has been working at the same university language centre in Canada for eight years. In November each year, he and all other long-term teachers have a professional development review meeting with the director of studies. Until now, Antoine has been sceptical about the usefulness of such meetings, but this time there is a new director of studies and she has asked teachers to use the EPG to assess themselves before the meeting. She will then discuss and ask questions about the self-assessment during their meeting.

Reflection as an aid to self-assessment

Self-assessment is more useful to teachers if it results from reflection, and stimulates further reflection. It needs to be based on evidence, which in this case means reflecting on experiences and events that back up the selection of one or other phase of development. For example, if a teacher refers to the descriptors in Figure 9.1 in order to help them determine whether they are at development phase 1.2 or 2.1 in assessment, they will need to reflect on their experience of assessing students' progress, and following up on progress assessment.

Development phase 1.2	Development phase 2.1
• can conduct and mark progress tests (e.g. end of term, end of year) when given the material to do so	• can conduct regular progress tests including an oral component
• can conduct oral tests when given the material to do so	• can identify areas for students to work on from the results of tests and assessment tasks
• can prepare and conduct appropriate revision activities	• can give clear feedback on the strengths and weaknesses identified and set priorities for individual work

Figure 9.1 Some descriptors relating to assessment

This will involve asking questions such as:

- What kind of progress tests do I give? Do I create them or are they provided by the textbook or the institutions?
- Do I also assess progress in oral skills? If so, what activities and materials do I use?
- What do I do after assessing progress? Do I prepare revision activities for areas where students are weak? Do I also give clear feedback to students individually and as a group, and suggest what they can do to improve in the areas where there are weaknesses?

Reflecting on these questions may lead to a realization that a more systematic or more individualized approach could be taken to assessing students' progress, or that, because the institution provides progress tests for teachers to use, there is a need to gain experience of developing the teacher's own progress tests or assessment activities, to complement those provided.

After deciding which development phase they are currently closer to, the teacher can usefully reflect on how to improve their practice. For example, by reflecting on the following questions:

- What sort of oral assessment tasks could I use with my students at B1 level? Where can I get ideas from? Is there a colleague who could help me with this, or could a colleague and I work together to produce assessment tasks that we can both use?

- How do I provide feedback to individuals after a progress test or assessment task, and how constructive is this feedback? How much help does each student get in understanding the feedback I give and in using it to improve their language knowledge and skills?

Activity 9.8

Using the descriptors in Figure 9.2, Pedro is assessing whether he is at development phase 2.1, 2.2, or 3.1 in language awareness. What questions would he need to reflect on before deciding? If he decides that he is currently at development phase 2.2, what questions is he likely to reflect on about his future practice?

Development phase 2.1	Development phase 2.2	Development phase 3.1
• can give correct models of language form and usage appropriate for the level concerned, except at advanced levels (C1–2)	• can give correct models of language form and usage for all levels up except at C2 on almost all occasions	• can select and give correct models of language form and usage on almost all occasions at all levels
• can give answers to questions about the target language appropriate for the level concerned, except at advanced levels (C1–2)	• can recognize and understand the language problem that a learner is having	• can answer almost all language queries fully and accurately and give clear explanations
	• can give answers to questions about the target language that are appropriate for the level concerned except at C2	• can use a range of techniques to guide learners in working out answers to their own language queries and correcting their errors

Figure 9.2 Some descriptors relating to language awareness

Reflecting on details of individual descriptors

A point that can be made about many of the descriptors in the EPG, especially those in the sections on key teaching competences and enabling competences, is that they often require more reflection than is at first apparent. Let us take just one example from development phase 2.2 of 'interaction management and monitoring': 'can provide/elicit clear feedback' (see Figure 6.4 on page 86). This descriptor may seem straightforward at first, but in practice it can be challenging to be able to do this successfully. What would teachers need to be able to demonstrate in order to claim they can do this? There are several questions teachers would need to be able to answer for themselves:

- What feedback was needed in the context of the activity: was it feedback about the language the students used, their success in carrying out the task, the quality of their responses, or something else?
- How did I provide or organize that feedback on language? Did I do it in a way that enabled students to learn from the feedback; for example, by eliciting clear examples and/or writing some up on the board?
- When I elicited feedback from students themselves, was it useful and clear? Did I repeat or get someone else to echo that feedback?
- Did I provide too much feedback or too little, and was it given at the right moment?
- How did the students feel about the feedback I provided?

This example demonstrates the usefulness of focused observation and self-observation (to be explored in the companion volume in this series *Language Course Management*). Observers can add value in teacher development by occasionally focusing on such questions, and teachers themselves can benefit from sometimes looking in detail at what they are doing by watching themselves at work. Ultimately, students themselves may be the best judges of whether feedback is useful, clear, and memorable; so asking them for their feedback can be very useful if it is done in the right way.

Considering different approaches to self-assessment

Regardless of whether teachers decide to do a complete self-assessment using the whole EPG or a partial self-assessment using only certain categories or subcategories of it, self-assessment can be done in two ways:

- by referring to a PDF version of the EPG and using a blank grid such as the one in Appendix 1 (see page 157) to record the assessment
- by using the online version of the EPG, the e-Grid (see Website references).

Teachers need to decide whether they will use the whole EPG or just some parts of it. As mentioned in 'Frequency of self-assessment' on page 113, this will depend on how much time they have and possibly also on whether they are doing the self-assessment in consultation with someone else who may later observe them and/or discuss the self-assessment with them.

The key part of self-assessment is the reading of each of the descriptors, reflecting on evidence from experience that helps decide which descriptors best apply at this time, and recording the relevant phase of development for the subsection being considered. Once the self-assessment is recorded on the blank grid, teachers will have an opportunity to review and possibly to amend their record. The profile may well look uneven; it is very unlikely that a teacher will be at the same development phase in every category, or in every subcategory in a given category. **Jagged** competence profiles are normal; they tell their story about perceived strengths, and where further development is desirable or necessary.

Once the self-assessment record is complete, teachers can begin to reflect on their future development plans: looking at the record, what seem to be the priorities, and how can the teacher identify the most suitable opportunities for development in these areas? What support is available from the institution and from colleagues, and what kind of plan can be worked out? The main priority is to be able to keep the record for a period (at least a year) and to be able to review development from time to time, possibly amending the development phases and dating the amendment, rather like a diary. Depending on their situation, teachers may need or wish to share their self-assessment record with managers or other colleagues.

Let us suppose a teacher, Caroline, has done a complete self-assessment using the e-Grid. A summary of the self-assessment is shown in Figure 9.3.

The summary, which includes brief information about Caroline and where she works, contains a profile of Caroline covering all the EPG categories in graphic form. This is where the jagged, uneven nature of the profile is most clearly visible.

Activity 9.9   Look at Caroline's profile in Figure 9.3. What could be the main reasons for why she feels less strong in some areas? If you were advising Caroline on her development, what would you suggest as priorities? What questions would you want to ask before making suggestions?

It seems Caroline has had little of her teaching assessed, which probably relates to the kind of pre-service training she did and her relatively short experience as a language teacher. She would be wise to request more observation and feedback, maybe even suggesting areas for the observer to focus on. She also has little confidence in her knowledge of assessment and skills in this area. Perhaps she has little opportunity or motivation to do more than use tests that she has been given by her institution. Considering that she feels she is quite good in the area of interaction management and monitoring, it is surprising that she is less sure about methodology. This may be another priority area for her, as is the use of digital media. Her low self-assessment in intercultural competence is probably due

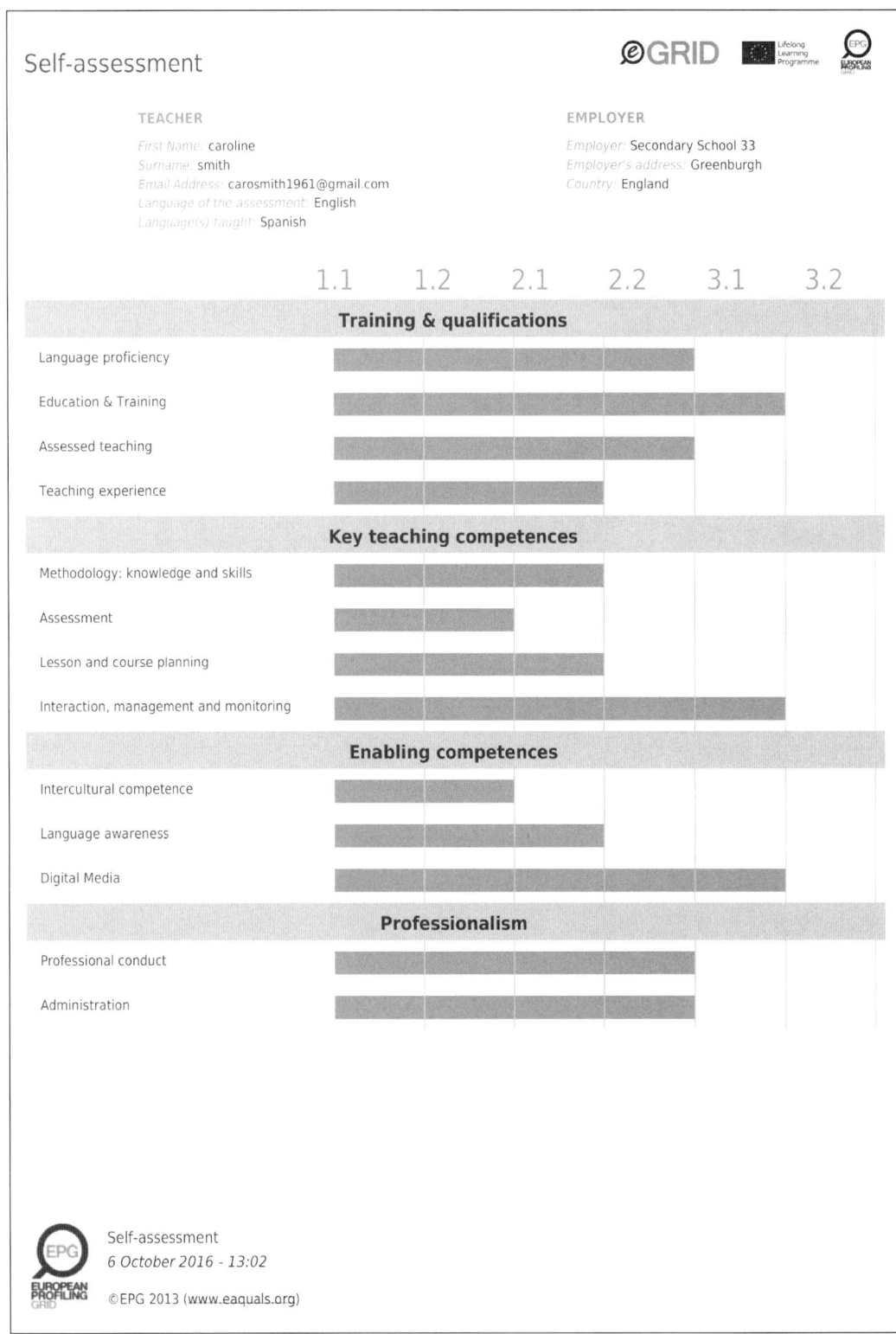

Figure 9.3 Screen showing the summary of a self-assessment

to the context she teaches in, but this competence is important in different ways in all contexts, so there will most certainly be scope for her to develop further in this area. Finally, it is clear from her profile that Caroline needs to be a little more disciplined when dealing with administrative tasks.

Teachers' views on using the EPG

The statements below come from teachers who have been using the EPG at an Eaquals-accredited centre for Spanish as a foreign language in Spain:

> '[The EPG] is a very useful tool for raising [our] awareness of the abilities and competences that a language teacher needs to be able to deploy.'

> 'If you don't know what the aim of doing [a self-assessment using the EPG] is, you may have doubts about being totally honest when filling it out, because you might feel that, if you don't assess yourself positively, you might give a negative impression of your capabilities.'

> 'It helped me to understand clearly where my weaknesses were.'

> 'In some categories, I wasn't sure in which phase of development to place myself.'

These four statements represent the range of views that teachers doing self-assessment might form of the process. It is not necessarily easy to be objective when doing a self-assessment, but it is important to remember that there are disadvantages in overestimating one's competences, and that being realistic is always the right policy when it comes to teacher development. On the other hand, it is also important for teachers not to think in terms of weaknesses but in terms of development needs and opportunities instead.

Flexibility is best

The EPG is a useful tool, but this does not mean it will work well for everyone. The purpose of the EPG is to encourage reflection and a degree of professional self-awareness, and thereby to stimulate teacher development. But there are situations in which it is unlikely to achieve this aim. The scenarios below illustrate some of these.

Sean is an experienced and creative teacher of English working in Dublin. In spite of much urging on the part of his director of studies, he almost never attends CPD workshops; and even when he was invited to lead one on creativity in the classroom, he refused. If he attends staff meetings at all, he does not participate. In an introductory workshop, the director of studies has encouraged all teachers to use the EPG for self-assessment, and most have done so, with some reporting back enthusiastically about the experience. Needless to say, Sean has not assessed himself.

| **Activity 9.10** | If you were Sean's manager, what steps would you take to try to persuade him to engage in self-assessment? What arguments do you think he would use to resist the idea? |

Such cases are difficult. Creative and charismatic teachers are popular with students and can point to this as evidence of their competence. Sean's manager could point to some areas in need of further development following an observation, such as the way in which he handles errors or illogical lesson organization, and perhaps refer to descriptors like those in the EPG. Another possibility would be to ask Sean to help a less experienced teacher who has assessed herself using the EPG and wants to discuss the outcome with someone. Of course, the danger is that she might be persuaded by Sean not to take any notice of the results but to concentrate on other aspects such as a sense of humour, games, and the use of creative resources, all of which are also potentially important. Perhaps a more effective way of helping Sean to self-assess is to accept that the EPG and similar tools are not (yet) for him, and to suggest that he video-records some of his teaching and discusses it with the manager and other colleagues.

Silvia is a very experienced teacher of Spanish working at a university language centre in Argentina. She read about the EPG in an article and assessed herself using the e-Grid. She was pleased to find that in almost all categories except assessment, she met the criteria for development phase 3.2. However, on further reflection she was concerned: did this mean she had reached the end of her professional development? She discussed her question with the centre manager, a firm believer in continuing professional development, even for very experienced teachers.

Activity 9.11   If you were the centre manager, what points would you have made? How would you have encouraged Silvia to move forward? What specific suggestions could you make?

This is not an uncommon problem with frameworks of competences like the EPG, especially in centres where there are several very experienced teachers. A difficulty with writing descriptors like those in the EPG is that they do not really indicate how well teachers are expected to deploy the competences referred to. Consider this phase 3.2 descriptor from the 'interaction management and monitoring' subcategory: 'can set up, monitor, and provide support to groups and individuals at different levels in the same classroom working on different tasks' (see Figure 6.4 on page 86). This is quite complex, as it involves managing groups of students at different levels, and different tasks for each group, at the same time. Teachers may believe they can do this because they have some experience of it, but how <u>well</u> can they do it? What kinds of tasks do they select or create? Above all, how well did these lessons work in retrospect? A way forward with Silvia might be to get her to focus on one area like this at a time, to sit down after a lesson where she has tried to address the needs of a mixed-ability group using different tasks, and to keep a reflective diary in which to record what worked and what did not. To what extent did the different groups benefit from the tasks? How does she know? How could the tasks have been made even more motivating and productive? How could the monitoring of groups have been even more effective? The key point is that in teaching (as in life), there is always, in retrospect, a better way of doing things, and lessons can always be learned for the future. Of course, the EPG does not cover everything, and it is possible to conceive of additional or alternative frameworks that provide descriptors for teachers who are on the way to being teacher trainers or managers of teachers.

Conclusion

In this chapter, we have discussed in detail the main benefits for teachers of using the EPG in its two formats. In order for the EPG to be useful as a tool for teacher development, teachers need to look for evidence in their practice to justify assigning themselves to a given development phase in each category of the EPG. This needs to be done regularly, for example every six or twelve months. It can also be done incrementally over the course of the year to reduce time pressure and to allow for specific categories to be focused on in turn.

It is important that the results of the self-assessment lead to some kind of plan of action which is somehow recorded. To formulate such a plan, it may well be useful to share and discuss the results of the self-assessment with a colleague. However, it has to be accepted that, in some situations, teachers may not feel comfortable engaging in self-assessment using tools like the EPG—in which case, other methods of self-assessment should be considered.

10 GUIDANCE ON USING THE EPG: TRAINERS AND MANAGERS

Introduction

The EPG is principally aimed at teacher development, and Chapter 9 explored the ways in which language teachers themselves could use it to aid their development through self-assessment and reflection. However, trainers, mentors, managers, and supervisors of language teachers all have a strong interest in encouraging and contributing to the development of the language teachers they work with. This chapter explores some of the ways in which these stakeholders in teacher development can use the EPG in their work with teachers.

Teacher trainers and mentors

The main role of teacher trainers is to foster and support teacher development, and to design and organize tasks and activities that offer opportunities for such professional growth. A distinction needs to be made between teacher trainers who work mainly in pre-service teacher education and those who are more active in the field of in-service teacher education, although many teacher trainers work in both fields. The focus of this chapter is mainly on those trainers working with practising teachers—that is, teachers who have already gained some teaching experience.

While teacher trainers generally work mainly on structured courses, mentors (who may themselves be trainers or simply more experienced teachers) generally work with individuals on an occasional basis while often continuing to teach themselves. Different institutions have different systems and names for them, but mentors are usually asked to help less experienced, or more recently appointed colleagues with their development through observation, feedback, co-planning, and being available to provide help. Mentors often see their duties as a welcome change from 'ordinary teaching' and a way of gaining experience that may later help them become more full-time teacher trainers.

Activity 10.1	What do you consider to be the main practical differences between the pedagogic methods used by a trainer of language teachers and those used by a language teacher? Are there areas where the approach and methods are similar?

To begin with the second question in Activity 10.1, there are clearly areas of overlap between the approach and methods of teacher trainers and those of teachers. Indeed, a type of teacher training called loop input (see Woodward, 2003) specifically builds on this overlap, as it involves teacher trainers using processes or techniques for training which are effectively the same as they expect their trainee teachers to use in teaching, although the content may well be different. This example is cited by Woodward: a teacher trainer wishes to introduce a technique for teaching which may be new for trainees, such as 'messenger dictation' whereby two students work together on a dictation, one memorizing parts of a text from a sheet posted on a wall in the classroom, then running back to the other, who writes down what the other dictates from memory. Rather than simply explaining the process, the trainer could have the trainees undergo it as if they were students, perhaps with a text making arguments for and against dictation. Experiential techniques like loop input provide trainee teachers with better opportunities to get the feel of an activity and reflect on it than would be the case if they just listened to the trainer describing it or watched a video clip of students doing it.

Other similarities with language teaching include the following:

- Trainers need to concentrate on skills, such as those relating to language awareness, and processes, such as giving feedback to learners, while at the same time helping trainees to understand and work on implementing these within a language lesson.

- Several aspects of communication need to be focused on in training; not just effective use of the target language but also use of the voice, body language, and the choice of good examples.

- Like language teaching, good teacher education combines raising awareness and understanding with practical activities—including, for example, tasks to be worked on in groups.

There are, however, several important differences:

- Language teaching focuses primarily on helping students to use the target language well in a variety of situations. It is mainly about the development of language knowledge and awareness, as well as language skills and the use of language for communication. Teacher training also focuses on knowledge, awareness, and skills, but these go well beyond language. As is made evident in the EPG, methodology, interaction management, how to plan, how to assess, and various other areas are all involved.

- Unlike language teachers, teacher trainers often find themselves observing and giving feedback on actual teaching. Language teachers seldom have the chance to observe their students communicating in the world beyond the classroom.

Teacher trainers working with practising language teachers are generally involved in one of three kinds of courses:

1 Courses that lead to a further qualification such as the **Cambridge English DELTA**, or the language teaching modules of a relevant MASTER's degree.

2 Courses that offer specialized training and development opportunities—for example, in using technology in language teaching, or teaching the language to specific groups such as very young learners, university students, or people working in business. These courses may lead to a certificate.

3 Courses organized in consultation with teachers themselves and their manager, which are designed to meet the needs of teachers working in a given institution. These courses may be obligatory or may be rewarded in some way, for example, with points in some kind of credit system.

Occasionally, trainers are employed by institutions to provide ad hoc or individualized support to teaching staff, especially newly appointed teachers and those with less teaching experience. More often, such work is done by mentors— colleagues who have more teaching experience, and who may also have teacher training experience and/or management duties as co-ordinators or supervisors. In such cases, each mentor may be responsible for supporting just one other teacher for a period of a few weeks or longer, or may work with two or three teachers over a longer period. An advantage of this system is that mentors can tailor their support to the individual needs of their mentees. It is, however, important that institutions using mentoring for new and less experienced teachers put in place a clear and robust mentoring system in consultation with the teachers concerned, in order to ensure that it will work to the benefit of all, and that this system is carefully monitored. Mentoring systems are considered in more detail in the companion volume in this series *Language Course Management*.

Activity 10.2	From what you already know of the EPG, in what ways do you think teacher trainers or mentors could use it in their work with practising teachers?

The EPG user guide includes various scenarios highlighting the ways in which teacher trainers or mentors may find it helpful to use the EPG in their work. Some of these scenarios are expanded on and developed below.

1 Assessing individual teachers' performance

Teacher trainers working on longer courses lasting, for example, an academic year or a semester, can use the EPG to assess the competences of each individual teacher throughout the duration of the course. It is important to note, however, that assessments using descriptors in the 'key teaching competences' or 'enabling competences' categories of the EPG can only be done if the teacher trainer has opportunities to observe teachers in a real, simulated, or microteaching situation. A first step might be to ask each teacher to do a self-assessment (see Chapter 9), using relevant categories of the EPG. The self-assessments can then be compared with the records of lesson observations carried out by the trainer, together with notes from the feedback discussions following these observations. A further step could be a meeting to compare the teacher's self-assessment with the trainer's assessment, so that any differences of opinion can be discussed. It is not uncommon for teachers to overestimate their competence in some areas and underestimate their competence in other areas. Comparing the two assessments in the light of evidence from observations offers a way of bringing these discrepancies into the open. If records are kept of the self-assessment, the trainer's assessment, and the key points arising from discussions about them, this will provide a good basis for reviewing progress over the duration of the course, the ultimate outcome of which should be for teachers to progress from one phase of development to a higher one in the areas focused on.

Where teacher trainers are working on shorter courses of, say, 12–60 hours, or where the course is very intensive (for example, 100 hours or more in four weeks) a different approach would be needed, depending on the course content and the opportunities available for practice and observation. For example, if it is not possible to use 'real' students in teaching practice on a course, and this is mainly done in the form of peer-microteaching, whereby a teacher practises teaching other teachers pretending to be students in a simulated lesson, the 'students' may not react or respond in the same way as real students would. In such cases, asking trainees to do a self-assessment against relevant selected descriptors, and then comparing this with the teacher trainer's own assessment could be beneficial fairly early on in the course. In such simulated teaching practice, the other teachers observing a colleague while pretending to be students could also be asked to comment with reference to the relevant descriptors in the EPG on how successfully they think their colleague used the techniques or skills in question. This will be more beneficial if another such assessment based on the same descriptors and involving the trainer, individual trainee teachers, and their colleagues is done towards the end of the course as evidence of the progress achieved.

Such situations are tricky to handle, but they do offer good training opportunities: an important part of practical teacher training is helping teachers to become more aware of their classroom behaviour and habits, and to reflect on ways of modifying them where necessary or desirable. In both scenarios described above, a key step involves the trainer pointing to—or getting the teachers themselves to point to—the evidence for their self-assessments by giving concrete examples to support their view of themselves. This is, of course, much easier to do if the teacher and trainer are able to refer to video or audio recordings of lessons observed; but it can also be done from careful notes made by the trainer during the observations. The discussion can then conclude with the teacher trainer making suggestions as to how progress could be made and also, perhaps, highlighting specific points to focus on for the next observation and in their future teaching in general.

A similar but more individualized approach can be taken by mentors, whose work is normally spread out over a longer, less intensive period and may only involve periodic observations of lessons given by the teacher. Ideally these observations should be preceded by a preliminary discussion of aims and the lesson plan, and be followed by a feedback discussion. The way in which mentors suggest using the EPG will depend on whether the support they are providing their mentees focuses on specific areas or is more general. Brief meetings held periodically to review progress between observations can help to ensure momentum is maintained.

Activity 10.3	List three or four key questions that a mentor could use or adapt when discussing a mentee's initial self-assessment based on sections of the EPG.

2 Drawing up a collective profile of a group of teachers

Looking at profiles of individuals in a group of teachers undergoing training can be a useful means of comparing and identifying individual strengths and gaps so that these can be taken into account when planning training. There may be several points of similarity between the profiles, but there will almost certainly be some points of difference, too. These similarities and differences can be taken into account, for example, when assigning teachers to groups to work on a task together, or when pairing teachers to work together on planning a lesson or co-teaching parts of a lesson. This kind of collective profiling can be especially useful when the teachers undergoing training work together as colleagues in the same institution. For example, it can enable them to identify one another's strengths and decide who to turn to for support in specific areas they may feel weaker in, and can also help to build and reinforce working relationships. The information can also help with mentoring: mentors can be selected on the basis of their strengths meeting the needs of new and less experienced teachers, as revealed by the assessments of all members of the teaching team.

In 2015, a report was done on the use of the EPG on four successive initial teacher training courses leading to the Cambridge English CELTA run in Bulgaria. The purpose was to see whether, and if so how, the EPG could help both the trainees and the trainer to assess progress during the course. Participants included both practising teachers of English and people with no experience, and both native and non-native speakers of English. The study investigated the development of the teaching competences of participants during the course by comparing their levels of competence at the start of the course with the level they had achieved by the end of the course. It focused on the two central categories of the EPG, 'key teaching competences' and 'enabling competences', although the participants assessed themselves against the descriptors in all categories at the beginning and end of the courses. The report found that:

• By the end of the course, most trainees had progressed to phase 2.1 and 2.2 in the categories focused on, although three participants felt they were less successful than this in the areas of lesson planning and assessment.

- The greatest progress was made in the subcategories of 'methodology: knowledge and skills', 'lesson and course planning', and 'interaction management and monitoring', while the least progress was made in the subcategories of 'digital media' and 'assessment'.

- All trainees were highly motivated to do the self-assessment and trace their development. They found the e-Grid user-friendly, and it took them about 15 minutes to complete.

- In general, trainees showed no tendency to overestimate or underestimate their performance (based on a comparison between self-assessments and trainer assessments).

The results of the study enabled the trainers to gain a clear idea of how trainees on the courses developed in relation to one another as the course progressed. Where there were areas that seemed generally to be causing problems, it led to certain aspects of the course programme being redesigned, such as increasing the time spent on background and practical aspects of assessment and the use of digital media. It also gave trainees collective experience of self-assessment that they seemed to find useful, and, it is to be hoped, may lead to a self-assessment habit as their careers continue.

3 Designing and running in-service teacher training programmes

The results of assessments based on the EPG can serve as a useful starting point when designing INSET programmes for groups of teachers, especially when the assessments have been compared with self-assessments and discussed with the individuals concerned. For example, if the self-assessment and assessment outcomes both indicate that some teachers experience difficulties with, or lack confidence in, setting up and managing group or pair work (see the 'interaction management and monitoring' subcategory), the trainer or mentor can plan additional focused observations followed by feedback discussions, and suggest that these teachers observe more experienced colleagues who have greater expertise and confidence in this area, and that they do some relevant reading prior to further discussion of the issue.

Activity 10.4	Three experienced teachers work as mentors in a large institution where there is a team of 16 language teachers. Their work is overseen by a teacher trainer, who also acts as a mentor. The mentoring team has recently arranged for all teachers to evaluate their competence in student assessment, an area which the institution sees as a development priority and a means of gaining competitive advantage. The results revealed that half the teachers do not feel confident in preparing tasks and tests related to CEFR descriptors to be used to assess students' progress towards achieving the next CEFR level.
	What training events and mentoring activities would you suggest for these teachers?

The outcome of the evaluation exercise described in Activity 10.4 is not surprising: generally, little attention is paid to the topic of student assessment in pre-service teacher education, perhaps because it is thought that assessing students' progress and achievement in language learning is mainly the responsibility of the institution and external examining bodies. However, especially in institutions where there is greater variation between the teaching programmes used by teachers working with students at similar levels, there is a need for teachers to regularly assess their students' progress using tasks and tests that relate to their specific teaching programme and the needs of their students.

A first step towards remedying the issue that the teachers in Activity 10.4 are having would be to ensure that they have all thought through what student assessment means, and how the various types (such as assessment for placement purposes, assessment of progress, and assessment of achievement) differ. They also need to be aware of and discuss examples of different means of assessment (such as tests, quizzes, oral tasks, and continuous assessment). Reading and discussing chapters of relevant books or articles on the subject may help to raise awareness. Another important assessment-related activity for all teachers working with teaching programmes that refer to external scales of language proficiency, such as the CEFR, is standardization training. Useful activities might include:

- sorting can-do descriptors into levels on a scale, as well as into categories (such as spoken interaction and spoken production)
- discussing recorded samples of student interaction or production to decide which level of proficiency the students have attained, and a similar activity with samples of student writing
- sorting items taken from listening or reading comprehension activities into the appropriate levels.

Only after sensitizing teachers to the types of evidence that are needed to determine the degree of progress that has been made and the differences in performance implied by the respective levels of proficiency is it reasonable to ask teachers to develop assessment tasks and tests for their own students. Once some sensitization and standardization work has been done, workshops can be organized to guide teachers in pairs or groups in preparing appropriate tests and tasks for assessing their students' progress, and to stimulate discussion on how and when these should be used, how they can be assessed or graded reliably, and how the results should be fed back to students and used to inform future teaching.

4 Adjusting teacher training programmes

The EPG levels of competence descriptors can provide useful insights for checking the design of existing teacher training programmes, including those for pre-service teacher training, and making adjustments where necessary. For example, deciding what phase or phases of development the teacher training is aimed at, and reviewing the competence descriptors for these phases, can extend and enhance the scope and aims of the teacher training programme by, for instance, identifying a need to deal in a more systematic way with intercultural issues and digital media (see the intercultural competence and digital media subcategories). The EPG can also help trainers make decisions about how much assessed teaching or teaching practice to include. In addition, the programme may seek to promote a self-assessment culture by encouraging trainee teachers to use parts of the EPG for reflection and action planning, as in the Bulgarian study on page 127.

5 *Encouraging the development of specific competences*

Assessing teachers using the descriptors in the EPG can make it easier for mentors and teacher trainers to guide individual work on areas of special interest or need. For example, if a teacher is particularly interested in issues of methodology and theories of learning (see the 'methodology: knowledge and skills' subcategory), they could be encouraged to do some further reading and to prepare a session for colleagues which goes into these topics in depth and aims to raise collective awareness of how different methods relate to individual learning styles and preferences. The teacher could also be encouraged to plan and carry out some classroom research with colleagues and perhaps write an article about their findings. Similarly, the EPG descriptors on language awareness and assessment could serve as stimulus for a teacher who is known to be good at explaining and modelling language, or skilled in using a specific assessment code for errors in written work to run a practical workshop on these topics. Inviting teachers with known strengths to contribute actively to INSET can boost morale and develop a stronger team ethic.

Activity 10.5   If you are a teacher trainer or mentor, would you find it helpful to use the EPG in your context to support your work? If so, in what ways would you be able to use it?

If you are not a teacher trainer or mentor, consider whether you think using the EPG could be helpful in teacher training and mentoring, and, if so, in what ways.

Managers of teachers

Language teachers are managed in different ways depending on how the institution where they work is structured. Mainstream schools and colleges normally have a language or languages department, with a head of department in charge, possibly assisted by an assistant head or co-ordinators for each language. Private language schools may have a director of studies or an academic manager responsible for overseeing the language programmes, perhaps with the support of co-ordinators for languages, levels, or age groups (adults, children, business clients, etc.). Many members of the management staff may find the EPG useful as a tool in carrying out certain aspects of their responsibilities relating to the management of teachers. For example, as has been discussed, the fundamental purpose of the EPG is to support and aid teacher development, which is a key area of responsibility for anyone managing teachers, as well as for teacher trainers, mentors, and indeed the teachers themselves. Many managers in language education are also responsible for facilitating the development of their teachers by organizing INSET and CPD opportunities, observing lessons, giving feedback, and carrying out assessments.

| **Activity 10.6** | Look at the list of responsibilities relating to the management of language teachers below. Based on your experience (as a manager or teacher, or in another relevant capacity), rank the responsibilities in order of importance (1 = most important) from the point of view of a) teachers and b) their employers.

a) Assigning teachers to classes and levels, as well as to non-teaching duties, i.e. deciding which teachers do what kind of work
b) Maintaining and providing training in the use of teaching equipment
c) Overseeing the provision of support for teacher development at individual and team level
d) Observing and giving feedback on teaching
e) Selecting, recruiting, and inducting new teachers
f) Ensuring teaching and assessment materials are available
g) Managing performance including review and appraisal
h) Establishing and reviewing procedures for record-keeping, dealing with teacher absence, handling students with special requirements, etc.
i) Proposing and consulting on systems for performance management, career progression, and teacher welfare
j) Other (what?)

Of the responsibilities listed in Activity 10.6, the EPG can provide help with a, c, d, e, and g. Again, the EPG user guide offers various suggestions and scenarios for managers who are considering using the EPG to help them fulfil their responsibilities. Adapted and expanded versions of these are provided below.

1 Creating reports on a team of teachers

Managers can use the e-Grid to create a collective profile of the teaching team, adding and removing assessments and self-assessments to it as and when necessary. An especially useful feature of the e-Grid in relation to collective profiling is the option to generate a report which presents teachers' profiles in two different ways:

• A report by teacher, which presents profiles of the teachers who have been assessed in numerical form, side by side, as seen in Figure 10.1. This report enables managers to see at a glance which teachers have stronger profiles or more developed competences in certain areas.

• A report by competence, which presents profiles in line with the order of categories in the EPG, as shown in Figure 10.2. This report enables managers to select a category of competence and see which teachers have reached which development phase in that category.

Jean Dupont		Juliane Henri		Marianne Martin	
TRAINING & QUALIFICATIONS		**TRAINING & QUALIFICATIONS**		**TRAINING & QUALIFICATIONS**	
Language proficiency	1.1	Language proficiency	3.2	Language proficiency	3.2
Education & Training	2.2	Education & Training	3.2	Education & Training	3.2
Assessed teaching	3.2	Assessed teaching	1.1	Assessed teaching	3.1
Teaching experience	1.2	Teaching experience	3.2	Teaching experience	2.2
KEY TEACHING COMPETENCES		**KEY TEACHING COMPETENCES**		**KEY TEACHING COMPETENCES**	
Methodology: knowledge and skills	2.2	Methodology: knowledge and skills	3.1	Methodology: knowledge and skills	3.1
Assessment	3.1	Assessment	1.2	Assessment	2.1
Lesson and course planning	2.2	Lesson and course planning	2.2	Lesson and course planning	1.1
Interaction, management and monitoring	1.1	Interaction, management and monitoring	3.2	Interaction, management and monitoring	3.1
ENABLING COMPETENCES		**ENABLING COMPETENCES**		**ENABLING COMPETENCES**	
Intercultural competence	2.2	Intercultural competence	3.2	Intercultural competence	1.2
Language awareness	2.1	Language awareness	3.2	Language awareness	2.2
Digital Media	3.1	Digital Media	2.1	Digital Media	1.2
PROFESSIONALISM		**PROFESSIONALISM**		**PROFESSIONALISM**	
Professional conduct	2.2	Professional conduct	2.2	Professional conduct	3.1
Administration	1.2	Administration	2.1	Administration	3.2

Figure 10.1 Report by teacher

Activity 10.7   Consider the two versions of the report on a small team of teachers in Figures 10.1 and 10.2. If you were the manager of these teachers and looking at these reports for the first time, what would you consider to be the development priorities for individuals and for the whole team?

2 *Employing new teachers and balancing the teaching team*

Selecting new teachers for the beginning of the academic year or for summer courses is a common challenge for managers. It may be relatively easy to attract candidates, but identifying those who will complement and strengthen the team as a whole is not so straightforward. If the EPG is habitually used for self-assessment in an institution, and if these self-assessments are reviewed in discussions with trainers, mentors, or managers and kept up to date, then an overview of the strengths and areas for development across the team can be created (see the previous section on 'Creating reports on a team of teachers'). This can be used to draw up a specification of the kinds of teacher they wish to recruit; for example, to work with certain types of students at an advanced level, or to participate in the development and use of digital media.

A collective profile of the teaching team also enables managers to see at a glance where specific areas of expertise need to be added. Many institutions prefer to have a teaching team in which different levels of experience and expertise are present: a situation where all teachers are at development phase 3.1 or 3.2 in most areas and have 10–20 years of experience might seem advantageous, but may actually not be beneficial from the point of view of the internal dynamics of the team. A range of

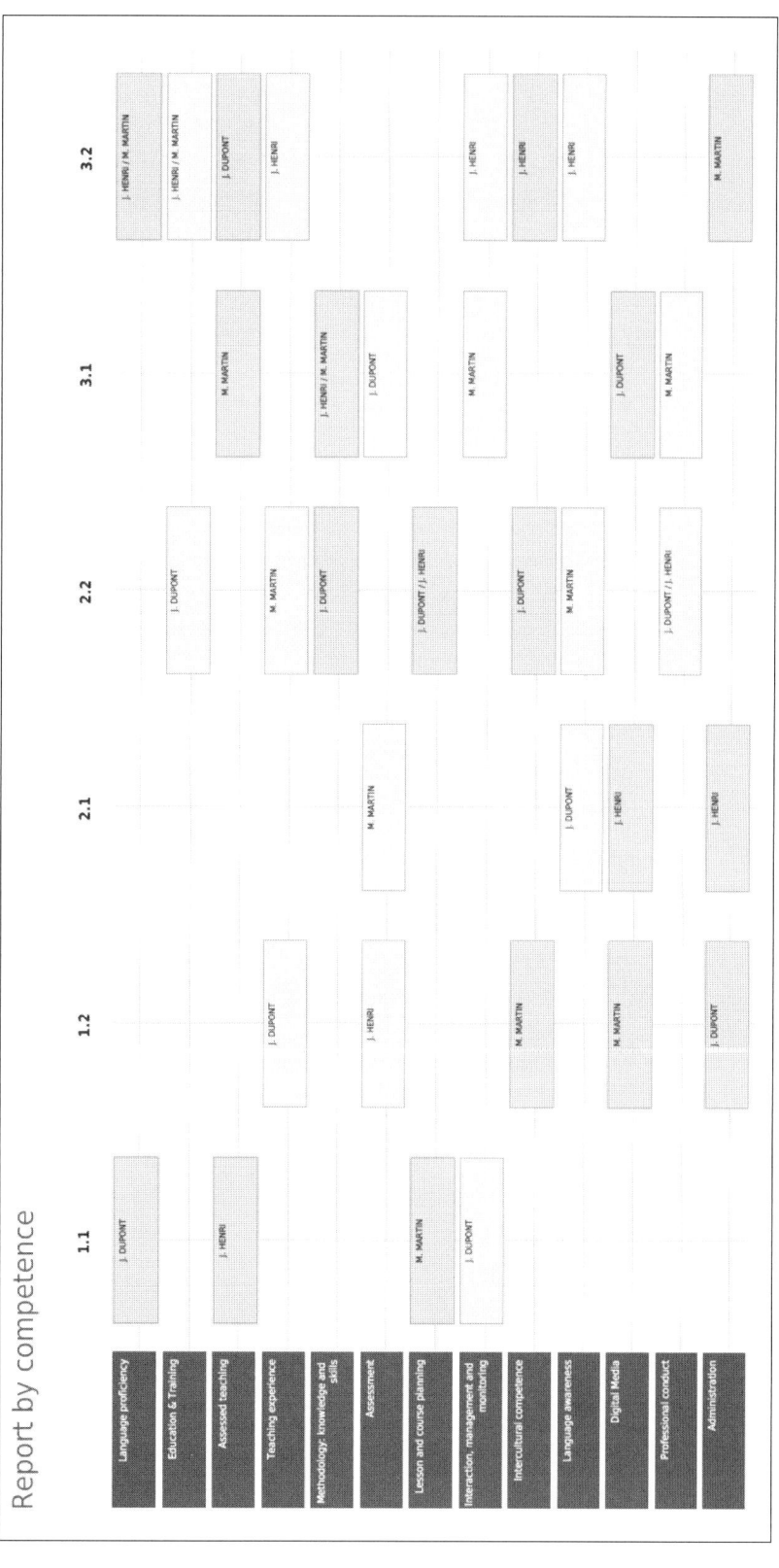

Figure 10.2 Report by competence

ages, levels of experience, and phases of development may in fact be better for the students, as well as the employer and the teaching team itself. For example, some institutions providing language courses for adults of different age groups consider it advantageous to have some teachers who are fairly close in age and life experience to their students. Diversity of ages and teaching experience can also be beneficial from a human resources perspective, as it helps to establish a clearly defined career progression structure within the institution. It is also useful to have some teachers who are especially interested and expert in specific areas—for example, assessment or intercultural competences—so that they can provide support and even leadership in these areas.

3 Matching teaching competences to course types

Managers are often faced with the task of choosing the best available teacher to take responsibility for a group with specific needs: for example, to teach a group of company employees, for which the teacher may need to have more developed skills and experience in the areas of planning, methodology, or the use of digital media; or to teach a group preparing for an advanced public language examination, for which well-developed language awareness and experience of the examination may be required. Reviewing and comparing the profiles of members of the teaching team will enable managers to make an informed decision about who is the best available teacher for each group.

4 Supporting performance management and appraisals

It is good practice in education, as in other professions, to establish systems for regularly reviewing employees' performance. A common approach in many organizations is to hold annual or biannual appraisals with each long-term employee. For teachers, preparation for the meeting usually involves some kind of self-review to list the things that have gone well and not so well since the previous appraisal, as well as considering objectives or priorities for future development to discuss with the manager. In the case of language teachers, self-assessment using the EPG has been found to provide useful additional input for the appraisal. As well as generally reviewing performance and the contributions teachers have made to the institution, managers and teachers can review the self-assessment together, discuss areas where there may be differences of opinion—especially where, in the view of the manager, teachers have overestimated or underestimated their level of competence—and use it to identify priorities for individual development to focus on until the next appraisal. If a self-assessment using the EPG was also done prior to the previous appraisal, the manager and teacher can discuss the progress made and ways in which doing the self-assessment has enhanced the work of the teacher individually and as a member of the teaching team.

During the appraisal, priorities for the institution can also be highlighted. For example, the institution may be facing the prospect of having to deal with unusually diverse groups in which many different nationalities, educational cultures, and religious backgrounds are represented. The discussion could focus on the teacher's interest in being deployed to teach one of these groups and on developing their intercultural competences in line with the descriptors in that section of the EPG in preparation for this challenge.

5 Supporting teacher development

In order to decide on priorities and budgets for different forms of CPD, managers have to identify the strategic and practical needs of the institution, as well as explore and assess the current competences and needs of individual teachers. For example, for strategic and competitive reasons, there may be a focus on raising the general level of qualifications within the teaching team in line with the 'education and training' and 'qualifications' subcategory of the EPG, and also bearing in mind the 'professional conduct' subcategory. Individual profiles of teachers based on self-assessment using the EPG will highlight their stronger and not so strong areas, and relevant discussions with each teacher will reveal their level of enthusiasm and readiness to participate in further training, for example at postgraduate level. Such analysis and discussion using the EPG can also assist managers in deciding how best to provide support for the professional growth of teachers; for example, by offering financial support to aid with course fees, allowing teachers time off for independent study, or enabling them to participate in specialist courses and/or attend national or international seminars and conferences.

The case study below comes from an academic manager at a school of Spanish as a foreign language who has been using the EPG with teaching staff in order to guide individualized teacher development as well as CPD in a 'tailored' manner, and is beginning to ask candidates for temporary teaching positions to do self-assessments as part of the selection process.

> 'I have used the EPG to make a global assessment of the academic team in order to enable us to offer individualized internal or external (e.g. Instituto Cervantes or other) training and development to each teacher, taking account both of the needs revealed through individual self-assessment and the more global needs of the team revealed by considering the self-assessments of all team members. In 2016, teachers again assessed themselves using the EPG, as a result of which, in addition to the above objectives, the professional development of teachers can be tracked both by each teacher and by me, which further enhances the professional development of teachers. In addition, this year we are asking candidates for summer teaching jobs to complete a self-assessment using the EPG as part of the selection process ... [I found it important] to make it clear to teachers that they must complete the self-assessments as honestly as possible. To do this, they need to understand exactly why we are using it and what its real function is. It is therefore important when assessing the results to bear in mind their subjective and relative aspects, depending on the different personalities and values of the various teachers.'

As this academic manager mentions, in order for the self-assessments done by teachers to provide background and guidance for teacher development, teachers need to undertake the process thoughtfully and honestly. This in turn implies that the manager needs to ensure that the EPG and the way it is to be used in the institution are clearly introduced and openly discussed so that teachers understand the potential benefits.

Themes relating to managing and supporting language teachers are dealt with in greater detail in the companion volume in this series *Language Course Management*.

6 Evaluating teachers' performance

Figure 10.3 shows an evaluation carried out by a manager. There is space for the manager's signature and an institutional stamp at the bottom of the form. This is so that the profile can be used as a formal record, for example when the teacher leaves that institution. It can also be used to accompany a job application. This is a potentially useful and attractive feature for teachers who are employed on short-term contracts but have the opportunity before leaving to complete a self-assessment and discuss it with their manager. Once it has been reviewed by and discussed with the manager, and any necessary adjustments have been made, the profile generated can serve as a valuable evaluation of the teacher's performance during their employment, as well as provide the teacher with a useful addition to their CV when applying for their next job—a kind of evidence-based reference. Whether it is used in this way will, of course, be a decision for the teacher.

It has to be recognized that not all employers will dedicate so much time and energy to supporting teacher development. Sometimes, it is simply the case that the workload of the teaching staff is too heavy or that there is a lack of resources—for example, too few co-ordinators or potential mentors. This need not mean that teachers cannot support their own and one another's development—or indeed that managers cannot promote and support bottom-up development activities. Managers could encourage teachers to engage in self-assessment using the EPG (as outlined in Chapter 9) or another tool (see Chapters 3 and 11), and then to find a way to discuss this with a colleague who has also done a self-assessment. The impact of such self-help discussions is likely to be greater, of course, if the teachers have been able to observe one another or have recorded themselves teaching and are also willing to discuss these samples of their teaching with colleagues. In the absence of institutional support, self-help development groups are a good alternative, and the EPG and similar instruments can be used at least as a means of stimulating group reflection and at best as a tool for setting an agenda for collective and individual self-organized development.

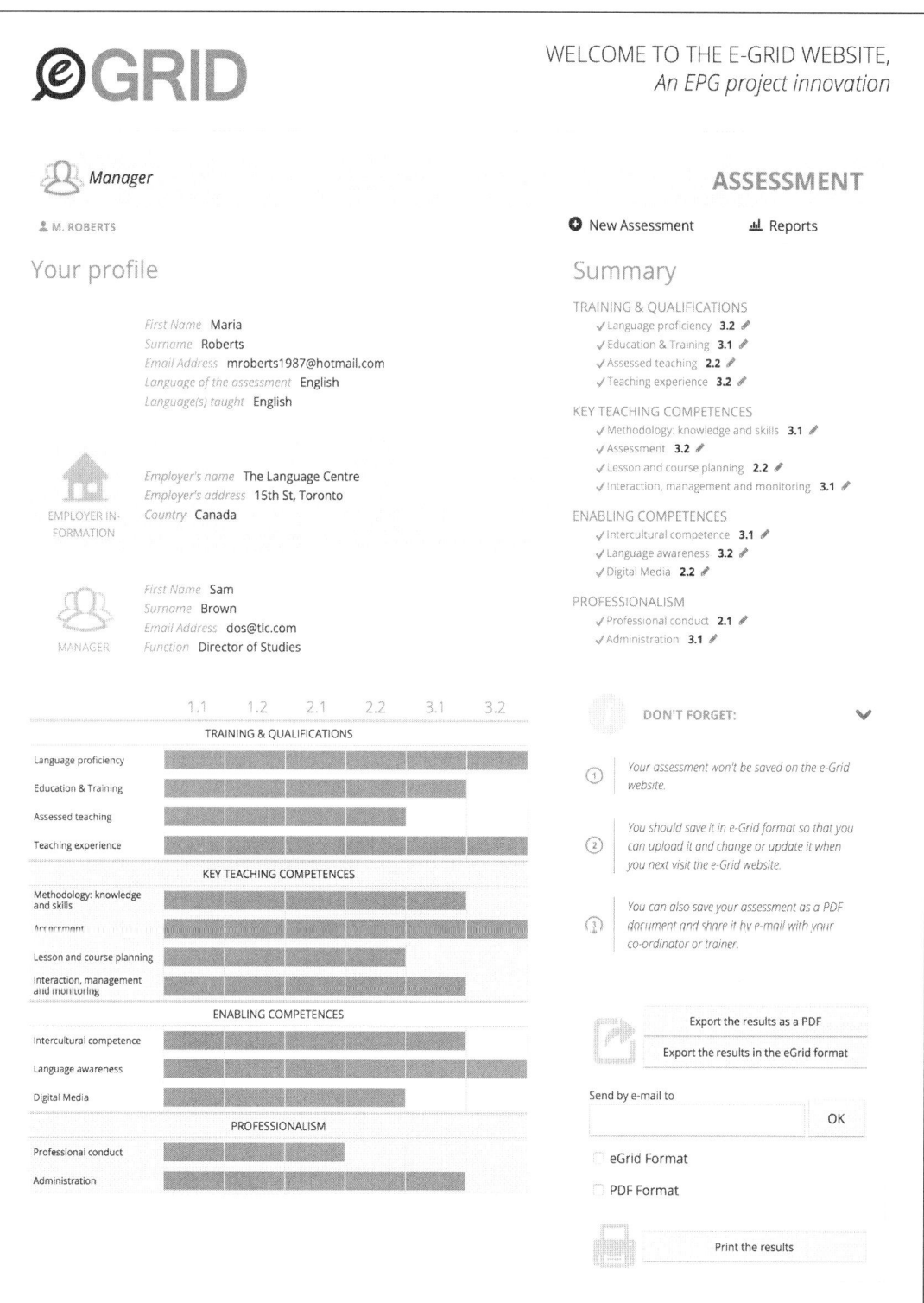

Figure 10.3 Evaluation screen

Conclusion

Assessing teachers' language teaching competences is important not only to stimulate and plan their professional development, but also for a variety of other reasons which have been explored in this chapter. For example in-service teacher trainers and mentors need to have a clear picture of the existing levels of competence and the development needs of the individual teachers they are working with; and they also require a means of assessing their further development over time, for example during and at the end of a course. Meanwhile, for managers and supervisors, an understanding of the strengths and capabilities of the members of their teaching team is essential in order for them to be able to assign teachers to appropriate courses and classes, and to discuss with them their professional development needs. Managers also need to have an overview of the competences and capabilities of the whole teaching team so that it can be managed sensitively and advantageously from the employer's point of view, and so that suitable new teachers can be recruited to complement the existing team when necessary.

The focus of this chapter has been on possible uses of the EPG for purposes like these by trainers, mentors, managers, and supervisors who are working with language teachers. It has, however, been emphasized that assessments of teachers by those in training, mentoring, or managerial roles are likely to contribute more effectively to teacher development and to the welfare of the institution if the assessments are compared with self-assessments by teachers using the same framework. Whatever differences there may be between the self-assessments and the teacher trainer's or manager's assessments can be explored in discussion with the teachers concerned and may be resolved on the basis of evidence from observed teaching. Where such support is not available, self-organized professional development stimulated by activities such as shared self-assessment, peer observation, and reading groups can go a long way towards increasing motivation and a sense of professional well-being, thereby improving students' experience of language learning.

PART FIVE

11 EAQUALS FRAMEWORK FOR LANGUAGE TEACHER TRAINING AND DEVELOPMENT

Introduction

Chapters 9 and 10 described in detail how the EPG can be used by language teachers, teacher trainers or mentors, and managers. This chapter provides details of a closely related but more extensive framework for language teachers which aims to build and expand on the EPG itself, and to bring together the best features of the various other frameworks considered in this book, notably in Chapter 3.

The roots of the **Eaquals Framework for Language Teacher Training and Development (Eaquals TD Framework)** (see Website references for a link where the framework can be downloaded for free) are to be found in the original Eaquals Profiling Grid, launched in 2006. Two years later, a new project group within Eaquals wanted to amplify the concise overview format of the Eaquals Profiling Grid, which then spanned only three pages, by developing an expanded version with more detailed descriptors for each of the main categories of competence. The idea was to create an additional tool that would be useful for designing INSET courses and events for practising teachers, and also to enable teachers and trainee teachers to assess themselves against more detailed, analytical descriptors. It is important to note, however, that the Eaquals TD Framework is in some senses a work in progress. While the EPG descriptors were subjected to a validation process involving nearly 2,000 language teachers, 100 trainers, and 65 people in management positions, the more numerous descriptors in the Eaquals TD Framework have not yet undergone a full process of validation.

The special interest group formed in 2009 to create the Eaquals TD Framework began by reconsidering the very concept of competence, in order to ensure that the contents of the proposed framework were well grounded. (The concept of competence adopted in this book was discussed and illustrated in Chapter 2.)

| Activity 11.1 | Look at the following definitions of the word 'competence'. Which do you consider to be the most suitable in relation to thinking about the competence (or competences) of teachers? Why?

1 'The ability to do something successfully or efficiently.' (Oxford Dictionaries; see Website references)

2 '… units of a certain complexity, implicating the whole of the individual and linked to socially relevant tasks in the context of which they are activated; in these situations, they signify the mobilization of different resources which may be internal (… knowledge, skills, or attitudes) or external (the use of a dictionary, resorting to a mediator …).' (A Framework of Reference for Pluralistic approaches to Languages and Cultures (ECML, 2012); see Website references)

3 'A cluster of related abilities, commitments, knowledge, and skills that enable a person … to act effectively in a job or situation.' (Business Dictionary; see Website references)

4 'The personal attributes or inputs of an individual. They can be defined as the behaviours (and technical attributes where appropriate) that individuals must have, or must acquire, to perform effectively at work.' (Competence and Competency Frameworks; see Website references)

Where teachers and teaching are concerned, it is more complex than the first and third dictionary definitions in Activity 11.1 seem to suggest, as is recognized in the second definition from FREPA. Stimulating and supporting students' learning requires both knowledge of various kinds—for example, of the target language, pedagogic methods, learner psychology, relevant teaching and learning resources, and so on—and practical skills, such as presentation, organizing language practice, managing classroom activities, and dealing with questions and errors. It is also important not to overlook the teacher's own values and attitudes, as these inevitably influence how a teacher teaches. In addition, as the fourth definition in Activity 11.1 points out, competence is inherently personal: whether the knowledge and skills are used well in the process of teaching will depend on the teacher's personal qualities, such as patience, confidence, voice, their ability to ensure that their actions and behaviour as a teacher are right for the specific context in which they are teaching, the needs of their students, the specific aims of the lesson or course, and even the mood of the class at a particular moment in time.

Designing the Eaquals TD Framework

Apart from the greater detail and the more numerous descriptors, the main differences between the Eaquals TD Framework in its final form and the EPG that superseded the Eaquals Profiling Grid are outlined below.

Scope

Unlike the EPG, which was designed as a concise framework to allow for rapid self-assessment/assessment against global descriptors, the Eaquals TD framework covers in more detail all that is included in the EPG (except for the 'training and qualifications' category, which was intended to focus attention on aspects of a teacher's CV). Figure 11.1 provides an overview of the contents of the Eaquals TD Framework, each main area of which is divided into a number of subsections.

Main areas and their subsections				
Planning Teaching and Learning	**Teaching and Supported Learning**	**Assessment of Learning**	**Language, Communication and Culture**	**The Teacher as Professional**
1 Learning needs and learning processes 2 Curriculum and syllabus (the teaching and learning programme) 3 Lesson aims and outcomes 4 The lesson – tasks, activities and materials	1 Teaching methodology 2 Resources/ Materials 3 Interacting with learners 4 Lesson management 5 Using digital media 6 Monitoring learning 7 Learner autonomy	1 Assessment and the curriculum 2 Test types – selection, design and administration 3 Impact of assessment on learning 4 Assessment and learning processes	1 Using the target language effectively with learners 2 Applying the principles of the Common European Framework for Reference 3 Giving sound language models and guidance 4 Handling relevant cultural issues as part of language learning 5 Applying practical insights from linguistics and psycholinguistics	1 Self-assessment and teacher autonomy 2 Collaborative development 3 Exploratory teaching 4 Lesson observation 5 Professional conduct

Figure 11.1 Main areas and subsections covered by the Eaquals TD Framework (adapted from The Eaquals Framework for Language Teacher Training & Development, www.eaquals.org, 2016, p. 6)

As can be seen from Figure 11.1, the 'training and qualifications' subcategories of the EPG are divided into the 'planning teaching and learning', 'teaching and supporting learning', and 'assessment of learning' areas of the Equals TD framework; the 'language, communication and culture' area of the Eaquals TD framework encompasses the first two of the 'enabling competences' EPG subcategories (with 'digital media' incorporated into the 'teaching and supporting learning' area); and the 'professionalism' category of the EPG is expanded on in 'the teacher as professional' area of the Eaquals TD framework.

Development phases

The EPG followed the pattern of the Common European Framework of Reference (CEFR), whereby three levels of language proficiency (A, B, and C), each divided into two, are used to chart a learner's development. The six phases of development in the EPG encompass a gradual progression from trainee teacher to highly competent teacher. For the Eaquals TD Framework, it was decided to retain only three phases of development, partly in order to simplify the task of writing a large number of additional descriptors for three intermediate phases, which would have been difficult to distinguish between with sufficient clarity.

Overview of competences

In line with this simplified progression of development phases, it was also decided to try to summarize in a few sentences the degrees of competence and professionalism achieved by teachers at the three phases of development.

Activity 11.2   Write two sentences that you feel summarize the teaching competence of a skilled teacher who has accumulated ten or more years of experience. Then write two more sentences that summarize the competence of a novice teacher with two months of experience. Finally, write two sentences describing a teacher whose competence falls between these two extremes. Then compare what you have written with the summary descriptors in Figure 11.2.

Development Phase 1	Development Phase 2	Development Phase 3
Teachers at this level are competent replicators.	**Teachers at this level are aware practitioners.**	**Teachers at this level are expert facilitators.**
They have pre-service teaching qualifications and can follow models of good practice. They plan, teach and reflect on their teaching effectively, and are responsive to guidance and feedback.	They have greater confidence and show initiative in planning, delivery and evaluation. They are open to and aware of issues that arise in the learning and teaching process, and can independently identify and implement appropriate teaching strategies, seeking guidance as necessary.	They have mastered a broad range of skills and strategies related to learning and teaching processes. They are competent in curriculum and syllabus development, creating teaching materials and developing assessment tools for use by others. They can also provide informed and instructive guidance to other teachers.
Teachers at this level are engaged in the further development of their teaching skills in the context of systematic institutional development programmes.	Within an institutional environment conducive to professional development, teachers at this level have gained a clear understanding of the nature and value of continuing professional self-development, can identify their professional needs, and can set objectives for continued professional growth.	Teachers at this level understand the need for continuing professional development even at this high level of competence, and are fully engaged in this, both as learners and as trainers or mentors of less experienced colleagues.

Figure 11.2 Overview of language teacher competences from the Eaquals TD Framework (adapted from The Eaquals Framework for Language Teacher Training & Development, www.eaquals.org, 2016, p. 9)

The key sentences in the summary descriptors in Figure 11.2 are those in bold: teachers at development phase 1 replicate what more experienced colleagues and mentors do, or what is detailed in teachers' books and textbooks, and in that sense are not yet fully independent; this is in contrast to those at development phase 2, who can be considered aware practitioners; and finally, those at development phase 3 are experts as practitioners and also as facilitators, both in terms of their relations with their learners and with their colleagues. These summaries capture the essential differences between the three main phases of development, which relate to confidence as well as competence.

Attitudes and values

In line with the broad definitions of competence discussed earlier in this chapter and in Chapter 2, the Eaquals TD Framework contains a set of values and attitudes as shown in Figure 11.3. These are not organized across the successive phases of development but are seen as applicable to all language teachers, whatever their experience and accumulated competence. This is not to imply that values and attitudes cannot be learned or developed by teachers during their training and development—many people involved in teacher education and supporting teacher development would consider the discussion and fostering of such attitudes and values to be an important part of their work. However, it is true that teachers and the institutions they work in do not necessarily articulate these values and attitudes clearly or regularly; so the purpose of listing them in the Eaquals TD Framework is to stimulate discussion of them.

As can be seen in Figure 11.3, some of the values and attitudes included are seen as overarching, while others are organized under headings relating to four areas of the Eaquals TD Framework. The list does not aim to be fully comprehensive; rather, an attempt was made during the development of the Framework to create an open-ended list of what were regarded as the most important values and attitudes for teachers to commit to.

Activity 11.3	Read through the list of values and attitudes in Figure 11.3. Can you think of any other values and attitudes to add this list? Write them down in your own supplementary list. Are there any that you think should not be included, and if so, why not?

Several possible additions come to mind: for example, a belief that learners need to take responsibility for their learning, and that a teacher's main job is to guide and support that learning, not to direct and control it; and an understanding that learners learn in very different ways, and that a rigid approach to guiding and supporting learning is unlikely to help all students in a group.

Encouraging teachers to articulate their values and beliefs about teaching and learning is a useful part of their continuing professional development. This can be done by various means, and includes asking teachers to watch short video clips of teaching and then discussing with one another not just their opinions of the teaching, but also the reasons for those opinions (see Ramani, 1987).

Language teachers at all phases of development share the following values and attitudes:

- A positive attitude to diversity and differences among learners, and respect for the personal and cultural background of the learners
- A readiness to adapt teaching to make the best possible provision for learners with learning difficulties or other disadvantages
- A belief that learning is more effective when learners are aware of their aims and the progress that they are making
- A recognition of the values of the learning-centred classroom, the various roles played by teacher and learners and their related modes of interaction
- A realization that knowledge and awareness of the target language and sound methodology contribute to successful teaching and learning.

Learners' needs and planning	Teaching	Assessment	Language, communication and culture
• A concern with identifying the learning needs and wants of all learners, and a conviction that methodical planning will lead to greater learner achievement and satisfaction • A readiness to consult learners and involve them in the planning process, prompting feedback and adapting activities in response to this • A realization that planning needs to be flexible and that plans should be modified in the light of the learning process and learners' needs • An appreciation that there should be clear progression from one lesson to another with reference to the planned learning outcomes, and that remedial work is likely to be necessary to address areas where language development is progressing more slowly • Critical awareness of a range of possible resources and their sound exploitation with reference to learners' level	• A belief in the value of lifelong learning and development • A commitment to taking account of both individual and group learning needs • An open mind concerning methods and teaching techniques for guiding and supporting language learning • A belief that learners learn more effectively if they are actively involved in decisions about the learning process • A determination to enable all learners to achieve optimal progress in their learning	• A belief that assessment is an integral part of learning and teaching and therefore should be designed and used in a fair, transparent and coherent way • A commitment to implementing the principles of validity and reliability in test design, delivery, grading and feedback • An appreciation of the impact of assessment on the whole learning and teaching process (assessment for learning; assessment of learning) • A commitment to providing timely, accurate and meaningful feedback to learners on their progress and attainment • An appreciation of the role of self-assessment in enabling learners to actively engage in monitoring their own progress	• A commitment to promoting linguistic diversity, plurilingualism and pluriculturalism, and a respect for varieties of language • A belief in language and communication as instruments for social cohesion and mobility • A belief in the dynamism and creative potential of language in planning, teaching and learning • A belief in the educational value of language learning and understanding of other cultures • A recognition of the importance of the role of foreign language learning in cognitive development • An appreciation of the significance of differences among individuals in terms of the way they use language

Figure 11.3 Values and attitudes from the Eaquals TD Framework (adapted from The Eaquals Framework for Language Teacher Training & Development, www.eaquals.org, *2016, p. 8)*

Another means is for teachers to discuss and then agree or disagree with values and attitudes in a simple list like those in Figure 11.3, mixed with others that are more extreme or polarized.

Activity 11.4	Read the brief accounts below of four teachers who have differing values and attitudes towards students. What would you say to each of these teachers if they explained their particular views to you? Which of them do you agree with and which do you disagree with? Why?

- Roberto believes that the best way to get students to learn is to make sure that their errors are systematically corrected and explained by the teacher with the help of other students. He also focuses quite a lot on repetition, getting students to repeat his examples individually and/or in a whole group, and then to provide further examples.

- Teresa believes students learn best if they link the spoken word and the written word. She uses the board often to capture sentences that students have been using in oral communication, and she also uses dictation quite often.

- Miguel believes the teacher should remain in the background as much as possible. Having set up activities, he often gets on with marking or is simply available if students have questions about the language or the task. Some of these he doesn't answer, telling them to find out for themselves.

- Sara believes textbooks are not a good idea. She thinks that it is best to use the students' and her own thoughts, experiences, opinions, and occasionally items from the media, or objects from outside the classroom, as a basis for language learning, as well as photos and videos brought in by students.

Division of knowledge and skills

The descriptors in each key area of the Eaquals TD Framework are divided into two related groups. The first set of descriptors normally includes descriptors of knowledge, which includes understanding and awareness. The second are skills or practical abilities that teachers can use in their teaching. In both cases, ordered lists of knowledge and skills are used in place of can-do or knowledge descriptors. This is illustrated in Figure 11.4.

Language thread and glossary

Concordancing was undertaken to ensure that there was consistency of language in the descriptors within each of the three development phases and to highlight the progression implied from one phase to the next. This checking was based on a list of verbs and phrases that were defined as appropriate for the three successive phases, as in the example provided in Figure 11.5.

Key Area 1: Teaching methodology		
Development Phase 1	**Development Phase 2**	**Development Phase 3**
Knowledge of	**Knowledge of**	**Knowledge of**
• concepts and meta-language needed for handling simple explanations and answering basic language questions at lower levels • the notions of 'reception', 'production' and 'interaction' as key dimensions of language skills development • the impact of affective factors on learning • the main approaches, methods and techniques of language teaching, and their underlying principles	• key issues in learning theory relevant to language learning • the principles and rationale behind the selection and use of commonly used teaching approaches, methods and techniques • the role of cognitive and affective factors in the learning process and the development of language competence	• theories and research related to more specialized approaches and methods of language teaching (e.g. task-based learning, the lexical approach, cognitive and affective factors in learning, etc.)
Skills:	**Skills:**	**Skills:**
• using basic teaching techniques for developing receptive skills and encouraging productive and interactive communication • using a range of core techniques to present and promote practice and support learning of the target language (grammar, vocabulary and pronunciation) • using classroom language appropriate to the level of the learners	• effectively using different teaching/learning techniques for the development of receptive skills, and engaging in productive and interactive communication • efficiently setting up and running a wide range of classroom language learning activities and techniques, and monitoring their effectiveness	• using a broad range of teaching approaches and techniques effectively and flexibly to fully develop receptive and productive skills • evaluating the appropriateness of techniques for different teaching and learning situations, and creatively deploying a wide range of techniques

Figure 11.4 Knowledge and skills descriptors for the 'teaching methodology' subsection from the Eaquals TD Framework (The Eaquals Framework for Language Teacher Training & Development, www.eaquals.org, 2016, p.14)

Phase 1	Phase 2	Phase 3
Supporting learning processes	Consolidating/reinforcing learning processes	Extending learning processes

Figure 11.5 Consistency of language across the three development phases

Using the Eaquals TD Framework

The Eaquals TD Framework contains a useful set of examples of how the Framework can be used. Some of the scenarios attached to these examples are reproduced below.

1 Engaging in self-assessment

As with the EPG, one of the main intended uses of the Eaquals TD Framework is self-assessment. However, given its relative length and complexity, teachers and trainee teachers will almost certainly want to use the Framework selectively and gradually for this purpose, choosing one or two key areas for review on each occasion; and where ongoing support for development is available, supervisors, mentors, and trainers will want to suggest certain key areas for teachers to refer to when assessing themselves. As yet, there is no online interactive version of the Eaquals TD Framework, so teachers should choose a method of recording self-assessment results in whatever way works best for them. Whether teachers choose to work with a PDF version on screen or a printed copy, they can highlight the descriptors that are felt to be most relevant at the time of assessment. An example of a highlighted PDF is shown in Figure 11.6.

2 Lesson observation

Scenario 1

At a language centre in Poland, it has been decided to intensify the lesson observation programme by making more time available to co-ordinators and teachers to carry out focused observation and peer observation for a fixed period, in order to be able to agree with teachers on some priorities for CPD. Following a week of **buzz observations**, in which co-ordinators of adult and young learner groups observed every class for 20 minutes unannounced and compared notes on the overall strengths and gaps in competence that they identified, the observers have used the Eaquals TD Framework to design observation sheets for longer developmental observations. The headings focus on two main areas:

- planning, especially 'the lesson – tasks, activities, and materials' descriptors (key area 4 of the 'planning teaching and learning' main area)
- teaching, especially the 'monitoring learning' descriptor (key area 6 of the 'teaching and supporting learning' main area).

Time will also be made available for teachers to observe each other in pairs, using the same sheet.

Key Area 2:	Resources and materials	
Development Phase 1	**Development Phase 2**	**Development Phase 3**
Knowledge of	**Knowledge of**	**Knowledge of**
• the main kinds of learning resources and ways they can be used for a limited range of levels and types of learners	• the rationale and principles behind the design, sequencing and use of a range of learning resources, including digital and internet based media • the relationship between cultural content in learning resources and the social and cultural background of learners	• methods of evaluating a wide range of materials from different practical and theoretical points of view, taking into account degrees of linguistic and cultural authenticity • categories, genres and text types in language teaching and learning
Skills:	**Skills:**	**Skills:**
• using a limited range of published materials and other learning resources effectively • managing teaching / learning resources well in familiar teaching contexts/situations • using resources effectively following suggestions in a teacher's guide or course-book • creating simple learning materials in line with learners' interests and needs to complement other resources • basic techniques for using authentic materials in class • adopting a professional approach to copyright and indicating the source of materials	• adapting and using effectively a wide range of published and other learning materials, including digital resources • evaluating the suitability of learning materials for different teaching contexts, taking into account linguistic, cultural and cognitive aspects • selecting, adapting and designing teaching/learning materials for a range of teaching situations to optimise learning outcomes • using various resources effectively, including the board and body language, to optimise learning outcomes • adapting and using creatively Information & Communication Technology (ICT) to aid learning in and outside the classroom	• adapting or designing and using resources effectively for a broad range of teaching contexts • reviewing, evaluating and selecting materials and resources for use by the teaching team • creating additional materials based on authentic oral and written texts, including digital resources, and teachers' notes • mentoring and guiding colleagues in selecting, adapting and designing materials • developing and managing online learning management platforms(e.g. Moodle) in a blended learning context

*Figure 11.6 Sample self-assessment record with relevant descriptors highlighted (*The Eaquals Framework for Language Teacher Training & Development, *www.eaquals.org, 2016, p.15)*

Activity 11.5

Look at one of the key areas mentioned in scenario 1 and draft a possible observation checklist based on the descriptors it contains.

Having done this, what advice would you give the co-ordinators in scenario 1 about using the Eaquals TD Framework for lesson observation?

The Eaquals TD Framework was not designed primarily as a tool for observation, but it does offer suggestions as to how observation criteria or checklists can focus on specific areas of competence; and this can enable observers to identify strengths and areas for improvement. One way of using the Eaquals TD Framework for this purpose is to simply photocopy the relevant page and, during the observation, circle the descriptors that seem to be applicable, especially those under 'skills'. Where necessary, these descriptors can be numbered, and related points for feedback can be recorded on a separate sheet.

3 Planning in-service training

Scenario 2

A school in Turkey has received a report from an accreditation body which has recently inspected it. The teaching met the required standard; but the report contained recommendations relating to aspects of learner assessment, the language proficiency and awareness of teachers, and increasing teachers' motivation and commitment. The director has now asked a working group that includes two teachers to refer to the Eaquals TD Framework, especially the sections on assessment of learning, the teacher as professional, and language, communication, and culture, in order to plan a series of professional development activities that will act on these recommendations.

Here, as in scenario 1, the Eaquals TD Framework is used is as a reference tool. The working group would first need to examine the accreditation body's recommendations, and then identify the relevant descriptors in the sections of the Eaquals TD Framework highlighted by the school director, of which there are many. Based on this initial analysis, they will be able to work out what phase of development to aim for. This may involve supporting a majority of teachers to progress from development phase 1 to 2, or from phase 2 to 3 in the areas identified as priorities; or this may depend on the area, with teachers aiming for a lower phase of development in assessment than in other areas because they were at a lower phase in assessment to begin with.

4 Mapping in-service training courses

Scenario 3

An institution runs numerous teacher refresher courses in the UK for teachers of English coming from across Europe on EU grants, and from countries beyond. The courses are well advertised, but the descriptions of content and structure are largely derived from previous courses, with considerable freedom being given to trainers to plan courses as they see fit when participants arrive.

In response to feedback from some participants and sponsors, the head of teacher training has been asked to use the Eaquals TD Framework for reference to organize the courses over three levels aimed at less and more experienced teachers, and to relate the aims and contents of the various courses to the Framework's areas and descriptors.

Activity 11.6
Look at the description of course aims below relating to a intensive 40-hour in-service course for practising language teachers run by the institution in scenario 3.

1 Increase participants' understanding of what works in the classroom to improve students' learning.

2 Help participants to:
- apply principles of expert teaching in the classroom
- improve the quality of teaching and learning outcomes in their own institutions
- gain a greater understanding of social, linguistic, and cultural diversity, and enhance participants' ability to work with this diversity
- increase their ability to address the needs of individual learners, including gifted learners and those with learning differences or disabilities
- improve their awareness of the target language and the cultures associated with it.

3 Raise participants' awareness of opportunities for professional and career development.

What steps would be necessary to enable you to relate these aims and the content of the course itself to the areas and descriptors in the Eaquals TD Framework in the way illustrated in scenario 3?

To do Activity 11.6 properly requires more details about what the course contains, i.e. what areas of knowledge and skill it will cover. The aims exemplified in Activity 11.6 seem to encompass almost all the areas dealt with in the Eaquals TD Framework, so the first step would be to decide where the main emphasis should be: on teaching and supporting learning, or planning teaching and learning, or both? Another important decision concerns the phase of development to be aimed for, which will depend on the phase of development that a majority of participants are already at when they start the course. A 40-hour course on its own is unlikely to enable participants to progress in any area from one broad phase of development to the next, unless they are almost there when they begin the course. This is why some institutions, such as the Instituto Cervantes in Spain, clearly categorize their courses for practising teachers according to the three successive phases of development in the EPG, which are those used in the Eaquals TD Framework.

The use of the Eaquals TD Framework for **mapping** INSET course content has become popular with some course providers for language teachers, for example Oxford University Press with its Oxford Teachers' Academy online courses, and the Norwich Institute for Language Education with its face-to-face and online courses for teachers. There are two main purposes behind this kind of mapping. The first is to check whether the coverage of the course content is appropriate given its main aims. By checking the skills and knowledge covered in the course against the descriptors in the Eaquals TD Framework, providers can identify gaps in the coverage or course plan that may need to be filled, as well as potential issues concerning order and priority. Mapping also helps the provider to ensure that the aims and content of the course are in line with the current phase of development of the intended participants. This is not to claim that the Eaquals TD Framework—or indeed any of the other frameworks featured in this book—is the only suitable reference tool available; in fact, the process of mapping can reveal gaps in the Framework itself. But having a tool like the Eaquals TD Framework, containing descriptors of language teachers' knowledge and skills organized over successive phases of development, makes mapping easier and more insightful. In this sense, there is a clear similarity with the way in which the CEFR is used for mapping the aims and contents of language courses.

Another important outcome of mapping is that providers are able to advertise their courses more objectively, clearly, and with greater confidence, in a way that the intended participants will find helpful.

Conclusion

This chapter has provided a brief overview of the Eaquals TD Framework, which offers detailed descriptors for the areas that are covered in a more generic manner by the EPG, while following similar principles. It is intended to enable teachers, trainers, and managers to go into greater detail in their assessment or self-assessment, which can be especially useful for those involved in teacher education and INSET. The greater level of detail of the descriptors in the Eaquals TD Framework, albeit distributed across just three phases of development, also makes the Framework a useful tool for more analytical planning and mapping of INSET, and observation. One way of looking at the Eaquals TD Framework is as an expanded supplement to the EPG, allowing teachers and those who support them to drill down into the areas of competence that are covered in the EPG.

12 FINAL CONSIDERATIONS

Diversity of competence frameworks

This book has explored the meaning and importance of language teaching competences, and the roles that frameworks of competences can play in helping language teachers to develop professionally. Chapter 3 considered the thinking behind and purposes of a number of different frameworks of competence, aimed primarily at language teachers. The remaining chapters focused mainly on the EPG and, in the case of Chapter 11, on the Eaquals TD Framework. All of the tools explored in this book have various features in common: they present key areas of teaching competence as tables of descriptors, many of them in the form of can-do statements like those in the CEFR; they cover a range of classroom-related skills, but also knowledge and skills related to other aspects of teaching and teacher development, such as knowledge of the subject (in most cases the target language), intercultural competences, the professional aspects of a teacher's work outside the classroom, and, in the case of the EPG, even their training and qualifications.

There are, however, important differences too. Only one or two, including the Eaquals TD Framework, contain descriptors concerned with a teacher's values and attitudes, which are an integral aspect of the concept of competence underpinning this book but are more difficult to describe as simple descriptors. Some frameworks are general in scope, while others focus on specific kinds of teaching and learning, for example in a university classroom setting or CLIL context. Some, such as the AITSL and LLUK frameworks for teachers of any subject and the European Profile looked at in Chapter 3, are more concerned with setting standards teachers or teacher trainers should adhere or aspire to than with self-assessment and professional development, while others, including the EPG, are intended primarily to map out and support individual teachers' professional and career development. It is partly for this reason that the EPG and other frameworks like it include scales of descriptors organized over three, four or six phases of development or career stages, a feature which, in a sense, provides a development pathway for teachers.

In summary, it is clear that there are many ways of mapping out, creating, and using such competence frameworks. In due course, those that already exist will be further developed and expanded or superseded, and new frameworks will be created for specialist areas or specific aspects of teaching.

Uses of competence frameworks

The main purpose of this book was to explore how frameworks and descriptors of teachers' knowledge and awareness, skills, and attitudes can be used by teachers and those working with them to further their individual and collective professional development. Much depends, however, on who is actually using the given framework and for what purpose. If teachers are using a framework for self-assessment and as a means of reflecting on their own competence, are they using it voluntarily and autonomously, or because they have been told to do so as part of an institution-wide professional development objective? If trainers, mentors, or managers are using the framework with the teachers or trainees they work with, is their purpose primarily to set professional or quality standards or, in certain cases (as in the BALEAP scheme), to achieve accredited status? Or is their purpose simply to encourage further development? There is, of course, nothing intrinsically 'wrong' with using frameworks in any of these ways, provided teachers understand—and preferably have a say in—how they are used. It is, however, important to add some words of caution. The first concerns the kinds of misuse or misinterpretation that can undermine the principles underpinning competence frameworks in general. The second concerns the limitations of such frameworks.

Carrots and sticks

The frameworks reviewed in this book were all, so far as can be ascertained, designed at least in part to aid and encourage teacher development, as tools to help map out the knowledge and skills needed to be effective as language teachers or teachers in general, and to promote the view that different contexts require different competences and levels of expertise. The frameworks are thus resources that propose to teachers and those working with them certain behaviours and areas of understanding that are necessary or desirable, depending on the context in which they are working and the needs of their students. The frameworks reviewed, the EPG and the Eaquals TD Framework in particular, are not intended to be used to put pressure on teachers, or to provide a set of **attainment targets** which create a link between attainment of competences and promotion or pay progression. In other words, the frameworks are not intended to be used by employers primarily as solutions to performance management.

There is an analogy here with some of the unintended uses to which the CEFR has been put in certain contexts. The CEFR proposes a series of levels of language proficiency illustrated by descriptors, which has proved useful because such a set of scales was previously not available. Thus language examination boards have used them to calibrate the levels of examinations and grades (an intended use); but by extension, some governments, especially in Europe, are using the levels as criteria for awarding or refusing citizenship or residency to applicants from outside Europe, and even as criteria for allowing or refusing permission for family reunion in cases where foreign nationals have been granted residency in a country and now want a spouse and/or their children to join them. This was definitely not what the creators of the CEFR or the Council of Europe, the mission of which includes upholding human rights, had in mind when proposing these scales. Similarly, most creators of frameworks for language teachers, especially those with successive phases or stages of development, do not wish their tools to be used to pressurize teachers against their will. As was mentioned in Chapters 9 and 10, institutions that wish to promote the use of a given framework such as the EPG should first work with teachers to agree on ways of using it which will most successfully aid their development, for the benefit of all key stakeholders: the teachers themselves, their students, and their employer. In short, the framework should inform and incentivize teachers or trainee teachers, not put pressure on them or create obstacles for them to overcome.

The parts and the whole

'The whole is greater than the sum of its parts' is a dictum usually attributed to Aristotle. During the development of the Gestalt theory of psychology, one of the psychologists involved, Kurt Koffka, amended the dictum to 'the whole is <u>other</u> than the sum of its parts'. Whatever the value of frameworks of competences for teacher development, it is clear that they are both analytical in nature and incomplete, as is shown by the fact that, while the frameworks that have been considered overlap with one another, they are all different and often complementary, but are not comprehensive in the sense that they cover all aspects of teaching in whatever context or specialist area. In each framework except FREPA (which concerns curriculum development in education), the process of teaching is analysed or broken down into individual skills or abilities that are linked to specific areas of knowledge and understanding, and supported in some frameworks by certain attitudes and values. But this atomistic or fragmented view of teaching is difficult to relate to teaching as teachers and their students actually experience it, or as observed by a supervisor, mentor, or trainer. The skills that teachers use in the classroom interact and interweave with each other and are deployed in a complex and dynamic manner that is influenced by teachers' personal qualities and characteristics, as well as by various factors specific to the teaching context. In this sense, the whole act of teaching is quite different from the various elements and behaviours described in the frameworks.

The important implication of this fact is that attention needs to be paid just as much to teaching as a holistic experience as to individual teaching competences. After all, students experience teaching holistically, and the effectiveness of it depends less on the knowledge teachers have or their individual skills and abilities than on the ways in which these are integrated, combined, and applied at a given moment in time. Working with the 'whole' teacher is a theme that is returned to in the companion volume in this series *Language Course Management*.

Conclusion

Teaching is complex and multifaceted, so it is not surprising that different organizations and individuals have developed such a variety of descriptions of it from different points of view, or have focused on certain aspects or special areas of language teaching rather than seeking to embrace the whole field of language education. Nevertheless, an important use of any framework of teaching competences, like those discussed in this book, is to stimulate the kind of reflection and self-assessment that takes teachers beyond their everyday duties and reality towards activities that foster positive professional development and contribute to their growth, as a whole teacher and as a whole person.

APPENDIX 1

BLANK GRID FOR SELF-ASSESSMENT OR ASSESSMENT

TEACHER'S NAME: DATE:

		DEVELOPMENT PHASE 1		DEVELOPMENT PHASE 2		DEVELOPMENT PHASE 3	
		1.1	1.2	2.1	2.2	3.1	3.2
TRAINING AND QUALIFICATIONS	Language proficiency						
	Education & training						
	Assessed teaching						
	Language teaching experience						

KEY TEACHING COMPETENCES	Methodology: knowledge and skills						
	Lesson and course planning						
	Interaction management and monitoring						
	Assessment						

ENABLING COMPETENCES	Intercultural competence						
	Language awareness						
	Digital media						

PROFESSIONALISM	Professional conduct						
	Administration						

THE EUROPEAN PROFILING GRID

TRAINING AND QUALIFICATIONS						
Development phase	**1.1**	**1.2**	**2.1**	**2.2**	**3.1**	**3.2**
Language proficiency	• is studying the target language at tertiary level • has achieved B1 proficiency in the target language	• is studying the target language at tertiary level • has achieved B2 proficiency in the target language	• has gained a B2 examination certificate in the target language and has oral competence at C1 level	• has gained a C1 examination certificate in the target language, or: • has a degree in the target language and proven proficiency at C1 level	• has gained a C2 examination certificate, or: • has a degree in the target language and proven proficiency at C2 level	• has a language degree or C2 examination certificate plus a natural command of the target language or: • has native speaker competence in the target language
Education & Training	• is undertaking preliminary training as a language teacher at a teacher training college, university or a private institution offering a recognised language teaching qualification	• has completed part of her/his initial training in language awareness and methodology, enabling her/him to begin teaching the target language, but has not yet gained a qualification	• has gained an initial qualification after successfully completing a minimum of 60 hours of documented structured training in teaching the target language, which included supervised teaching practice or: • has completed a number of courses or modules of her/his degree in the target language and/or language teaching pedagogy without yet gaining the degree	• has a degree in the target language with a language pedagogy component involving supervised teaching practice or: • has an internationally recognised (minimum 120 hour) certificate in teaching the target language	• has a degree or degree module in teaching the target language involving supervised teaching practice or: • has an internationally recognised (minimum 120 hour) certificate in teaching the target language and also: • has participated in at least 100 hours of further structured in-service training	• has completed a master's degree or degree module in language pedagogy or applied linguistics, involving supervised teaching practice if this was not part of earlier training or: • has a post graduate or professional diploma in language teaching (min. 200 hours course length) • has had additional training in specialist areas (e.g. teaching the language for specific purposes, testing, teacher training)

Assessed Teaching	• is gaining experience by teaching parts of lessons and sharing experience with a colleague who is providing feedback	• has had experience of being supervised, observed and positively assessed while teaching individual lessons • has had experience of running teaching activities with small groups of students or fellow trainees ('micro-teaching')	• in initial training, has had a total of at least 2 hours of successful documented, assessed teaching practice at at least two levels • in real teaching has been observed and had positive documented feedback on 3 hours of lessons	• in training, has had a total of at least 6 hours of successful documented, assessed teaching practice at at least two levels • in real teaching has been observed and had positive documented feedback on 6 hours of lessons at three or more levels	• has been observed and assessed for at least 10 hours during teaching practice and real teaching at various levels and with different types of learner, and has received positive documented feedback on this	• has been observed and assessed for at least 14 hours during teaching practice and real teaching, and has received documented feedback on this • has been assessed as a mentor or observer of less experienced teachers
Teaching Experience	• has taught some lessons or parts of lessons at one or two levels	• has own class(es) but only experience at one or two levels	• has between 200 and 800 hours documented unassisted teaching experience • has taught classes at several levels	• has between 800 and 2,400 hours documented teaching experience: • at various levels • in more than one teaching and learning context	• has between 2,400 and 4,000 hours of documented teaching experience, including: • at all levels except C2 • in several different teaching and learning contexts	• has at least 6,000 hours documented teaching • has taught in many different teaching and learning contexts • has experience of mentoring/training other teachers

The European Profiling Grid © EAQUALS 2013 – Brian North, Galya Mateva, Richard Rossner and the EPG Project 2011–2013

KEY TEACHING COMPETENCES

Development phase	1.1	1.2	2.1	2.2	3.1	3.2
Methodology: knowledge and skills	• is learning about different language learning theories and methods • when observing more experienced teachers, can understand why they have chosen the techniques and materials they are using	• has basic understanding of different language learning theories and methods • can select new techniques and materials, with advice from colleagues • can identify techniques and materials for different texts	• is familiar with language learning theories and methods • is familiar with techniques and materials for two or more levels • can evaluate from a practical perspective the suitability of techniques and materials for different teaching contexts • can take into account the needs of particular groups when choosing which methods and techniques to use	• is well acquainted with language learning theories and methods, learning styles and learning strategies • can identify the theoretical principles behind teaching techniques and materials • can use appropriately a variety of teaching techniques and activities	• can provide theoretical justification for the teaching approach being used and for a very wide range of techniques and materials • can use a very wide range of teaching techniques, activities and materials	• has a detailed knowledge of theories of language teaching and learning and shares it with colleagues • can follow up observation of colleagues with practical, methodologically sound feedback to develop their range of teaching techniques • can select and create appropriate tasks and materials for any level for use by colleagues
Assessment	• can conduct and mark end of unit tests from the course book	• can conduct and mark progress tests (e.g. end of term, end of year) when given the material to do so • can conduct oral tests when given the material to do so • can prepare and conduct appropriate revision activities	• can conduct regular progress tests including an oral component • can identify areas for students to work on from the results of tests and assessment tasks • can give clear feedback on the strengths and weaknesses identified and set priorities for individual work	• can select and conduct regular assessment tasks to verify learners' progress in language and skills areas • can use an agreed marking system to identify different types of errors in written work in order to increase learners' language awareness • can prepare for and coordinate placement testing	• can design materials and tasks for progress assessment (oral and written) • can use video recordings of learners' interactions to help them recognise their strengths and weaknesses • can apply CEFR criteria reliably to assess learners' proficiency in speaking and writing	• can develop assessment tasks for all language skills and language knowledge at any level • can apply CEFR criteria reliably to assess learners' proficiency in speaking and writing at all levels and help less experienced colleagues to do so • can create valid formal tests to determine whether learners have reached a given CEFR level • can run CEFR standardisation

Lesson and course planning	• can link a series of activities in a lesson plan, when given materials to do so	• can find activities to supplement those in the textbook • can ensure coherence between lessons by taking account of the outcomes of previous lessons in planning the next • can adjust lesson plans as instructed to take account of learning success and difficulties	• can use a syllabus and specified materials to prepare lesson plans that are balanced and meet the needs of the group • can plan phases and timing of lessons with different objectives • can compare learners' needs and refer to these in planning main and supplementary objectives for lessons	• can plan a course or part of a course taking account of the syllabus, the needs of different students and the available materials • can design tasks to exploit the linguistic and communicative potential of materials • can design tasks to meet individual needs as well as course objectives	• can conduct a thorough needs analysis and use it to develop a detailed and balanced course plan that includes recycling and revision • can design different tasks based on the same source material for use with learners at different levels • can use analysis of learner difficulties in order to decide on action points for upcoming lessons	• can design specialised courses for different contexts that integrate communicative and linguistic content appropriate to the specialism • can guide colleagues in assessing and taking account of differing individual needs in planning courses and preparing lessons • can take responsibility for reviewing the curriculum and syllabuses for different courses
Interaction management and monitoring	• can give clear instructions and organise an activity, with guidance	• can manage teacher-class interaction • can alternate between teaching the whole class and pair or group practice giving clear instructions • can involve learners in pair and group work based on activities in a course book	• can set up and manage pair and group work efficiently and can bring the class back together • can monitor individual and group activities • can provide clear feedback	• can set up a varied and balanced sequence of class, group and pair work in order to meet the lesson objectives • can organize task-based learning • can monitor learner performance effectively • can provide /elicit clear feedback	• can set up task-based learning in which groups carry out different activities at the same time • can monitor individual and group performances accurately & thoroughly • can provide/elicit individual feedback in various ways • can use the monitoring and feedback in designing further activities	• can set up, monitor and provide support to groups and individuals at different levels in the same classroom working on different tasks • can use a wide range of techniques to provide/elicit feedback

ENABLING COMPETENCES

Development phase	1.1	1.2	2.1	2.2	3.1	3.2
Intercultural competence	• understands that the relationship between language and culture is an important factor in language teaching and learning	• is learning about the relevance of cultural issues in teaching • can introduce learners to relevant differences in cultural behaviour and traditions • can create an atmosphere of tolerance and understanding in classes where there is social and cultural diversity	• understands and is able to take account of relevant stereotypical views • can use own awareness to expand students' knowledge of relevant cultural behaviour, e.g. politeness, body language etc. • can recognize the importance of avoiding intercultural problems in the classroom and promotes inclusivity and mutual respect	• can help learners to analyse stereotypical views and prejudices • can integrate into lessons key areas of difference in intercultural behaviour (e.g., politeness, body language, etc.) • can select materials that are well matched to the cultural horizon of learners and yet extends this further using activities appropriate to the group	• can use web searches, projects and presentations to expand own and learners understanding and appreciation of intercultural issues • can develop learners' ability to analyse and discuss social and cultural similarities and differences • can anticipate and manage effectively areas of intercultural sensitivity	• can use her/his extensive knowledge of intercultural issues when this is appropriate to assist less experienced colleagues • can develop colleagues' ability to deal with cultural issues, suggesting techniques to defuse disagreements and critical incidents if they arise • can create activities, tasks and materials for own and colleagues' use and CAN seek feedback on these
Language awareness	• can use dictionaries and grammar books etc as reference sources • can answer simple questions about language that are frequently asked at levels she/he is teaching	• can give correct models of language form and usage adapted to the level of the learners at lower levels • can give answers to language queries that are not necessarily complete but that are appropriate for lower level learners	• can give correct models of language form and usage appropriate for the level concerned, except at advanced levels (C1-2) • can give answers to questions about the target language appropriate for the level concerned, except at advanced levels (C1-2)	• can give correct models of language form and usage , for all levels up except at C2 on almost all occasions • can recognize and understand the language problem that a learner is having • can give answers to questions about the target language that are appropriate for the level concerned except at C2	• can select and give correct models of language form and usage on almost all occasions at all levels • can answer almost all language queries fully and accurately and give clear explanations • can use a range of techniques to guide learners in working out answers to their own language queries and correcting their errors	• can always give full, accurate answers to queries from students about different aspects of language and usage • can explain subtle differences of form, meaning and usage at C1 and C2 levels

Digital Media					
• can use word-processing software to write a worksheet, following standard conventions • can search for potential teaching material on the internet • can download resources from websites	• can create lessons with downloaded texts, pictures, graphics, etc. • can organize computer files in logically ordered folders	• can use software for handling images, DVDs, and sound files • can use any standard Windows/Mac software, including media players • can recommend appropriate online materials to students and colleagues • can use a data projector for lessons involving the internet, a DVD etc.	• can set and supervise on-line work for learners • can use software for handling images, DVDs, and sound files	• can train students to select and use on-line exercises appropriate to their individual needs • can edit and adapt sound and video files • can show colleagues how to use new software and hardware • can coordinate project work with digital media (using, for example, a camera, the internet, social networks) • can troubleshoot most problems with classroom digital equipment	• can train students to use any available classroom digital equipment (IWB incl.), their mobiles, tablets etc. profitably for language learning • can show colleagues how to exploit the teaching potential of available digital equipment and internet-based resources • can design blended learning modules using a learning management system e.g. Moodle

PROFESSIONALISM

Development phase	1.1	1.2	2.1	2.2	3.1	3.2
Professional conduct	• seeks feedback on her/his teaching practice and other work • seeks advice from colleagues and handbooks	• acts in accordance with the mission and regulations of the institution • liaises with other teachers about students and lesson preparation • acts on trainers' feedback after lesson observation	• welcomes opportunities to share class teaching (team-teach) with colleagues at one or two levels • acts on feedback from colleagues who observe her/his teaching • contributes to the institution's development and good management and reacts positively to changes and challenges in the institution	• welcomes opportunities to be observed by managers and colleagues and receive feedback on teaching • prepares for and participates actively in professional development activities • actively participates in the development of the institution and its educational and administrative systems	• acts as mentor to less experienced colleagues • leads training sessions with support from a colleague or when given material to use • observes colleagues and provides useful feedback • when the opportunity arises, takes responsibility for certain projects related to the development of the institution	• creates training modules for less experienced teachers • runs teacher development programmes • observes and assesses colleagues who are teaching at all levels • organises opportunities for colleagues to observe one another
Administration	• completes routine tasks like taking the attendance register; giving out/ collecting/ returning materials	• delivers required plans and records of lessons correctly completed and on time • marks homework and tests efficiently	• handles marking and report writing efficiently • keeps clear, well-organised records of lessons • hands in documents and feedback by time requested	• handles administrative tasks around the job efficiently • anticipates regular but less frequent tasks and completes them in good time • deals with students' issues, enquiries, feedback appropriately	• coordinates administrative tasks with others; collates information, reports, opinions, etc. if asked to do so • takes responsibility for certain administrative tasks such as organising teachers' meetings, gathering, analysing and reporting on end of course feedback etc.	• acts as course coordinator if asked to do so • liaises with enrolment dept / finance dept / sponsors / parents etc. as necessary • contributes actively to the design or review of administrative systems

GLOSSARY

The definitions provided here reflect the way in which the terms are used in this book. In some cases, other definitions exist for use of the terms in other contexts.

appraisal: The process of assessing employees' (in this case, teachers') performance against expectations and/or objectives, often done through annual or more frequent meetings between individual employees and their managers.

assessed teaching: Teaching that has been observed and evaluated in a formal way by a senior teacher, mentor, or academic manager.

assignment: A task, often a written task, that students, especially university students, are asked to do as part of their course of study.

attainment target: An objective of learning or study that is usually formally laid down in the course programme.

autonomous learning: Learning that is organized and carried out by students, and takes place without the direct support of a teacher.

blended learning: A combination of face-to-face classroom methods with computer-mediated activities.

bottom-up: Processes, such as professional development, are described as 'bottom-up' if decisions are made by teachers rather than, for example by their managers.

British Association of Lecturers in English for Academic Purposes (BALEAP): A professional association that runs conferences and has its own specialized scheme for professional development in this field.

buzz observations: These are normally observations of a short part of a lesson which give the observer a 'snapshot' of the teacher's work. The time is usually not arranged in advance; the teacher only knows that they will be observed at some point during the day, or week.

calibrated: Matched with or measured against expectations or levels on a scale—in this case, the development phase for which descriptors were proposed.

Cambridge English CELTA: Certificate in Teaching English to Speakers of Other Languages, an initial training qualification for teachers of English offered by Cambridge English.

Cambridge English DELTA: Diploma in Teaching English to Speakers of Other Languages, an in-service training qualification for experienced teachers of English offered by Cambridge English.

certificate in teaching the target language: An official document which certifies that a person has successfully completed a structured course on teaching the target language; for example, see *Cambridge English CELTA*.

Common European Framework of Reference for Languages (CEFR): An internationally recognized framework which provides descriptors (can-do statements) for measuring language ability, prioritizing the communicative competences of learners of foreign languages at different levels (A1, A2; B1, B2; C1, C2).

competence: The ability to deploy a combination of relevant knowledge, skills, and attitudes in an appropriate way to successfully accomplish a given task, such as language teaching.

Content and Language Integrated Learning (CLIL): A kind of teaching programme in which students are taught a subject in a second or foreign language, thereby allowing them to improve their proficiency in the language at the same time as learning the content of the subject.

continuing professional development (CPD): The activities, experiences, and events that help groups and individuals (in this case, teachers and others in the field of language education) to develop professionally during the course of their employment.

Council of Europe: An international organization of 47 member states of Europe dedicated to human rights, democracy, and the rule of law that has its own language policy unit, which has contributed in great measure to European language education, for example through their preparation and dissemination of the CEFR.

course co-ordinator: The person responsible for the development and day-to-day operation of a specific language course.

critical thinking: The objective analysis and evaluation of an issue or topic in order to form a judgement about it.

curriculum: The overall description of the aims, content, length, organization, methods, and evaluation of an educational course.

degree module: A self-contained unit that is part of a degree course.

descriptor: A statement that describes a given competence, area of knowledge, or characteristic, usually presented in organized groups within a framework, such as the CEFR.

digital media: Digitized content (text, graphics, audio, and video) for teaching that can be transmitted over the internet or computer networks.

documented: Evaluative or factual information recorded in writing or another form.

domain: An area of practice or knowledge; for example, that of language education.

Eaquals: An international association of institutions and people that provide or are involved in language education. Eaquals, which stands for 'evaluation and accreditation of quality in language services', is committed to fostering excellence in language education.

Eaquals Framework for Language Teacher Training and Development (Eaquals TD framework): A framework of descriptors organized over three phases of development, which is designed to assist teachers in assessing their own strengths and identifying their development needs.

Education and Training 2020 strategy: The framework used among European Union member states for co-operation in education and training, which consists of a forum for exchanging best practice and expertise, and for gathering and disseminating information and evidence of what works, as well as providing advice on and support for policy reforms.

English for Academic Purposes (EAP): The teaching and learning of English for purposes related to university-level study of subjects through the medium of English.

European Centre for Modern Languages (ECML): A division of the Council of Europe that runs a programme of projects and events on language education.

European Language Portfolio (ELP): A system for enabling students of European languages to assess themselves against the self-assessment scales in the CEFR and to record their progress and achievements in language learning.

European Profiling Grid (EPG): A framework of descriptors available in a number of different languages to enable language teachers to assess themselves and create a 'profile' of their competences, and to help managers and teacher trainers assess language teachers. It is also available in interactive form online as the e-Grid.

examination certificate: A document that certifies a level of language proficiency, according to a set of agreed standards such as the CEFR.

feedback: Comments and opinions given, for example, by students to teachers during a course, or by teachers to students during or after a language activity, or by an observer to a teacher after watching a lesson.

focused observation: A form of lesson observation where the observer focuses on certain aspects, such as classroom management, handling of errors, etc.

group work: Classroom interaction which involves various groups of students simultaneously doing a task together.

ICT: Information and communication technology, a term commonly used to refer to digital resources and equipment such as those deployed in teaching.

incremental scale: A scale of levels or phases which are arranged in order of increasing grade.

indicator: A phenomenon, event, or state of affairs that provides evidence of or a measure for something else; for example, the quality of teacher training courses.

induction: Processes and information that help orientate a new employee or student in an institution.

in-service training (INSET): Training offered to an employee in the form of workshops or short courses, for example, that they can attend while working.

inspector: An official representing an external body who visits an institution, such as a school, to check the quality of its services and facilities against standardized criteria.

interactive whiteboard: A large interactive display that connects to a computer and projector.

jagged: Used in relation to competence profiles to describe those in which some levels of competence are much higher or lower than others.

jigsaw tasks: Tasks which require participants to put things in the right categories and/or order, often by physically moving pieces around.

language awareness: Knowledge about the target language (form, meaning, and use) and understanding of how the target language—and communication in general—works.

language learning theories: Accounts of the psycholinguistic, cognitive, and affective processes involved in learning a language and of the conditions that need to be met in order for these processes to take place.

language pedagogy: The principles and methods of instruction applied when teaching students a language.

language proficiency: The level of linguistic knowledge of a language and ability to use it.

learning management system: Software for the administration, documentation, tracking, reporting, and delivery of education courses or training programmes, for example Moodle.

learning strategies: A learner's approaches to learning and using information to learn; for example, the ways in which a learner attempts to work out the meanings and uses of words, grammar rules, and other aspects of the language they are learning.

learning style: A learner's individual and habitual ways of acquiring information and skills.

mainstream school: A school which provides basic primary and/or secondary education across the curriculum, often used in contrast with the term 'language school'.

mapping: The activity of relating something (such as a course programme for teachers) to something else (such as a framework of descriptors of teachers' knowledge and skills).

marking system: The use of different symbols to indicate a type of mistake made in written work; for example, *WO* for wrong word order, *S* for wrong spelling, etc.

mentor: An experienced teacher, tutor, or academic manager who shares knowledge, skills, and perspectives to support the personal and professional growth of a less experienced teacher.

microteaching: An approach in teacher training whereby trainees practise teaching for a short period of time with peers or volunteer students, usually with a trainer observing them.

mobile devices: Phones, tablets, and other computer devices that can be carried around and, in this case, used in classrooms.

models of language form and usage: Accurate and appropriate examples of language structures that students can imitate, practise with, and learn from.

modular: Having the characteristic of being divided into 'modules' or different units or areas, in this case areas of teaching competence.

needs analysis: A procedure for identifying why students need or wish to study the target language, including the purposes for which they will use it and in what specific contexts.

pair work: Classroom interaction which involves students working on a language learning task with a partner.

placement testing: The procedure for assessing the language level of students prior to starting a course in order to place them in the right group.

professional development: The professional growth that teachers achieve in the process of gaining experience and knowledge and reflecting on their teaching; see also *continuing professional development (CPD)*.

professional diploma: A document showing that a teacher has undergone assessment and successfully completed a teacher training or language course.

profile: A representation of the different levels and characteristics that define an individual in some way; in this case, the various levels of competence a teacher might have in different areas.

progress testing: A procedure designed to assess learners' developing language and skills in relation to the course they have been following.

reference sources: Materials which can be used for reference purposes, such as dictionaries, grammar books, teacher's books, encyclopaedias, etc.

reflection: The experience of considering the implications of something that has happened, a decision to be made, or a state of affairs. In this book, the term is used mainly to describe the kind of thinking teachers do after assessing themselves, following a lesson, or when thinking about their own development needs.

reflective practice: The process of reflecting systematically on what one does professionally, for example as a language teacher, in order to learn from the experience (see Wallace, 1991).

self-assessment: The process of assessing one's own performance or competence in general or in a specific context. In this book, it is used to describe the process of considering one's own knowledge and skills in relation to certain criteria.

self-observation: The process of reflecting systematically on one's own teaching after (and sometimes during) a lesson. Teachers can make notes and discuss their self-observation with someone else. It is, of course, far easier to do this if a video or at least an audio recording has been made.

staff development: Events and activities designed to help employees, in this case language teachers, to develop their skills and expertise in given areas; see also *continuing professional development (CPD).*

stakeholders: People with a specific interest or involvement in something, such as an institution providing language education. Stakeholders in this case can be students, teachers and other staff, and also parents, employers, local authorities, etc.

stereotypical views: Fixed and/or simplistic ideas that people have of a particular type of person, culture, way of behaving, etc.

syllabus: A written outline and summary of the content of a course of instruction and the order in which skills and/or knowledge are to be taught, usually including an indication of how the time should be allocated.

target language: The language which is being taught as an additional or foreign language.

teacher development: The gradual development of individual teachers' competences, including knowledge, skills, and attitudes, that takes place as a result of training, day-to-day teaching experiences, interaction with colleagues, training events, etc.

teacher education: Higher study specifically aimed at giving people the knowledge and skills to become teachers or to become more expert teachers. Teacher education commonly takes the form of a one- or two-year postgraduate course, or a specialized first degree course.

teacher trainers: Teachers or lecturers who work on teacher education and teacher training courses.

teacher training: Systematic courses, usually of a mainly practical nature, designed to enable people to teach, either generally or in a specific area.

teaching approach: The way in which a teacher or institution promotes and applies principles and methods of teaching.

Teaching Knowledge Test: A suite of tests offered by Cambridge English to test teachers' knowledge about different aspects of English language teaching.

teaching technique: A specific way of handling a classroom activity.

team-teach: To work with one or more colleagues to plan and teach language lessons for the same group of learners.

top-down: Processes, such as professional development, are described as 'top-down' if those in managerial positions make the key decisions on behalf of those they are managing.

trainee teacher: A person taking a formal course, often at a university, in order to qualify as a teacher.

Trinity CertTESOL: The certificate offered by Trinity College London as an initial qualification for teachers of English to speakers of other languages.

troubleshoot: To identify, analyse, and solve problems or faults, in this case in classroom equipment.

tutorial: A meeting between a teacher or university lecturer and a student or a small group of students to discuss the work that they are doing.

usage: The way language forms and vocabulary are actually used in speaking and writing.

validation: The act of ensuring that something is valid, i.e. that it is true to its purpose, in this case the process of ensuring that descriptors actually describe what they are intended to describe at the intended development phase.

WEBSITE REFERENCES

Chapter 3

The EAQUALS framework for language teacher training and development

www.eaquals.org/our-expertise/teacherdevelopment/the-eaquals-framework-for-teacher-training-and-development

Education and Training 2020 strategy (European Union)

http://ec.europa.eu/education/policy/strategic-framework

European Profile for Language Teacher Education: Main report

www.lang.soton.ac.uk/profile/report/MainReport.pdf

European Profile for Language Teacher Education: Appendices

www.lang.soton.ac.uk/profile/report/Appendices.rtf

European Portfolio for Student Teachers of Languages (ECML, 2006)

www.ecml.at/epostl

'Towards a Common European Framework of Reference for language teachers' Project (ECML, 2016)

www.ecml.at/ECML-Programme/Programme2016-2019

Cambridge English Teaching Framework (Cambridge English, 2014)

www.cambridgeenglish.org/teaching-english/cambridge-english-teaching-framework/

British Council Continuing Professional Development (CPD) Framework for teachers

www.teachingenglish.org.uk/sites/teacheng/files/CPD%20framework%20for%20teachers_WEB.PDF

European Framework for CLIL Teacher Education (ECML, 2011)

www.ecml.at/tabid/277/PublicationID/62/Default.aspx

BALEAP Competency Framework for Teachers of English for Academic Purposes

www.baleap.org/resources/baleap-publications

BALEAP CPD Accreditation Scheme Handbook: Teaching English for Academic Purposes (BALEAP, 2014)

www.baleap.org/accreditation/institutions

A Framework of Reference for Pluralistic Approaches to Languages and Cultures (ECML, 2012)

www.ecml.at/Resources/ECMLPublications/tabid/277/PublicationID/82/language/en-GB/Default.aspx

Chapter 4

European Profiling Grid (EPG)

www.epg-project.eu/the-epg-project

Common European Framework of Reference (CEFR)

www.coe.int/t/dg4/linguistic/Cadre1_en.asp

European Language Portfolio

www.coe.int/t/dg4/education/elp

European Profiling Grid – e-Grid

http://egrid.epg-project.eu

Chapter 6

Business Dictionary

www.businessdictionary.com

Oxford Dictionaries

www.oxforddictionaries.com

Chapter 11

Competence and Competency Frameworks: Resource Summary

http://www.cipd.co.uk/hr-resources/factsheets/competence-competency-frameworks.aspx

Eaquals TD Framework

www.eaquals.org/our-expertise/teacher-development/the-eaquals-framework-for-teacher-training-and-development

REFERENCES

AITSL (2011). *Australian professional standards for teachers.* (Copyright Education Services Australia, 2011.) Retrieved June 2016 from www.aitsl.edu.au/australian-professional-standards-for-teachers/standards/list

ALTE (2010). *The ALTE code of practice.* Retrieved June 2016 from www.alte.org/attachments/files/code_practice_eng.pdf

BALEAP (2008). *Competency framework for teachers of English for academic purposes.* Retrieved June 2016 from www.baleap.org/wp-content/uploads/2016/04/teap-competency-framework.pdf

BALEAP (2014). *Teaching English for academic purposes: CPD accreditation scheme handbook.* Retrieved June 2016 from www.baleap.org/wp-content/uploads/2016/04/TEAP-Scheme-Handbook-2014.pdf

Boyatzis, R. (1982). *The competent manager: A model for effective performance.* New York: John Wiley and Co.

British Council. (2015). *Continuing professional development framework for teachers.* Retrieved June 2016 from www.teachingenglish.org.uk/sites/teacheng/files/CPD%20framework%20for%20teachers_WEB.PDF

Cambridge English. (2014). *The Cambridge English teaching framework.* Retrieved June 2016 from www.cambridgeenglish.org/teaching-english/cambridge-english-teaching-framework

Chomsky, N. (1965). *Aspects of the theory of syntax.* Cambridge, MA: MIT Press.

Council of Europe (2001). *Common European framework of reference for languages: Learning, teaching, assessment.* Cambridge: Cambridge University Press. Retrieved June 2016 from www.coe.int/t/dg4/linguistic/Cadre1_en.asp

Council of Europe (2010). *Guide for the development and implementation of curricula for plurilingual and intercultural education.* Strasbourg: Council of Europe. Retrieved June 2016 from www.coe.int/t/dg4/linguistic/Source/Source2010_ForumGeneva/GuideEPI2010_EN.pdf

ECML (2006). *European Portfolio for Student Teachers of Languages.* Retrieved June 2016 from www.ecml.at/epostl

ECML (2011). *European framework for CLIL teacher education.* Graz: ECML.

ECML (2012). *A framework of reference for pluralistic approaches to languages and cultures.* Graz: ECML. Retrieved June 2016 from www.ecml.at/Resources/ECMLPublications/tabid/277/PublicationID/82/language/en-GB/Default.aspx

EPG Project (2013). *The European profiling grid and user guide.* Retrieved June 2016 from www.epg-project.eu/the-epg-project

European Commission (2013). *Supporting teacher competence development for better learning outcomes.* Brussels: EU Commission. Retrieved July 2016 from http://ec.europa.eu/education/policy/school/doc/teachercomp_en.pdf

Kelly, M., & **Grenfell, M.** (2005). *European profile for language teacher education: A frame of reference.* Retrieved June 2016 from http://www.lang.soton.ac.uk/profile/report/index.htm

Kelly, M., Grenfell, M., Allan, R., Kriza, C., & **McEvoy, R.** (2004) *European profile for language teacher education: A frame of reference.* UK: University of Southampton

LLUK (2007). *New overarching professional standards for teachers, tutors and trainers in the lifelong learning sector.* Retrieved June 2016 from www.et-foundation.co.uk/wp-content/uploads/2014/04/new-overarching-standards-for-ttt-in-lifelong-learning-sector.pdf

Mann, S. (2005). The language teacher's development. *Language Teaching, 38(3),* 103–118. Retrieved June 2016 from www2.warwick.ac.uk/fac/soc/al/staff/teaching/mann/mann_s/stateof.pdf

Ramani, E. (1987). Theorizing from the classroom. In *ELT Journal, 41/1,* 3–11.

Wallace, M. J. (1991). *Training foreign language teachers: A reflective approach.* Cambridge: Cambridge University Press.

Walsh, S., & **Mann, S.** (2015). Doing reflective practice: A data-led way. *ELT Journal, 69(4),* 351–362.

Wenger-Trayner, E., & **Wenger-Trayner, B.** (2015). *Communities of practice: a brief introduction.* Retrieved June 2016 from http://wenger-trayner.com/wp-content/uploads/2015/04/07-Brief-introduction-to-communities-of-practice.pdf

Woodward, T. (2003). Loop input. *ELT Journal, 57(3),* 301–304.

INDEX

Page numbers annotated with 'g' and 'f' refer to glossary entries and figures respectively.